Alexander Mackenzie

History of the Mathesons,

With genealogies of the various branches

Alexander Mackenzie

History of the Mathesons,
With genealogies of the various branches

ISBN/EAN: 9783337726591

Printed in Europe, USA, Canada, Australia, Japan

Cover: Foto ©ninafisch / pixelio.de

More available books at **www.hansebooks.com**

HISTORY

OF

THE MATHESONS,

WITH

GENEALOGIES OF THE VARIOUS BRANCHES.

BY

ALEXANDER MACKENZIE, F.S.A., Scot.,

Editor of the "Celtic Magazine;" author of "The History of the
Mackenzies;" "The History of the Macdonalds and
Lords of the Isles;" &c., &c.

O CHIAN.

INVERNESS: A. & W. MACKENZIE.
MDCCCLXXXII.

INSCRIBED

TO

LADY MATHESON OF THE LEWS,

AS A

TRIBUTE OF RESPECT FOR HERSELF, AND TO THE MEMORY

OF HER LATE HUSBAND,

SIR JAMES MATHESON, BART.,

BY

THE AUTHOR.

CONTENTS.

ORIGIN—AND BENNETSFIELD MATHESONS ... 1-34

THE MATHESONS OF LOCHALSH AND ARDROSS 35-48

THE MATHESONS OF SHINESS, ACHANY, AND THE LEWS 49-54

THE IOMAIRE MATHESONS 55-58

SIR JAMES MATHESON OF THE LEWS, BARONET 59-72

LIST OF SUBSCRIBERS.

AITKEN, Dr, F.S.A., Scot., Inverness
ALLAN, WILLIAM, Esq., Sunderland
ANDERSON, JAMES, Esq., Hilton, Inverness
BEST, Mrs VANS, Belgium—(3 copies)
BLAIR, Sheriff, Inverness
BURNS, WILLIAM, Esq., Solicitor, Inverness
CAMPBELL, GEO. J., Esq., Solicitor, Inverness
CARRUTHERS, ROBERT, Esq., of the *Inverness Courier*
CHISHOLM, ARCHD. A., Esq., Procurator-Fiscal, Lochmaddy
CHISHOLM, COLIN, Namur Cottage, Inverness
CHISHOLM, THE, Erchless Castle
CLARKE, JAMES, Esq., Solicitor, Inverness
CRAN, JOHN, Esq., F.S.A., Scot., Bunchrew
CROAL, THOS. A., Esq., F.S.A., Scot., Edinburgh
DAVIDSON, JOHN, Esq., Merchant, Inverness
FINLAYSON, RODERICK, Esq., Nairn
FOSTER, W. E., Esq., F.S.A., Aldershot—(2 copies)
FRASER-MACKINTOSH, CHAS., Esq., M.P., F.S.A., Scot.
FRASER, WILLIAM, Esq., W.S., Edinburgh
GRAY, HENRY, Esq., Bookseller, Manchester
HAMILTON, SEYMOUR, Esq., London
HORNSBY, JAMES, Esq., Gairloch Hotel
MACANDREW, H. C., Esq., Sheriff-Clerk of Inverness-shire
MACDONALD, ANDREW, Esq., Solicitor, Inverness
MACDONALD, JOHN, Esq., Merchant, Exchange, Inverness
MACDONALD, KENNETH, Esq., F.S.A., Scot., Town-Clerk of Inverness
MACDONALD, LACHLAN, Esq. of Skaebost
MACKAY, JOHN, Esq., C.E., Hereford—(4 copies)
MACKAY, WILLIAM, Esq., F.S.A., Scot., Solicitor, Inverness
MACKAY, WILLIAM, Esq., Chamberlain of the Lews
MACKENZIE, Captain COLIN, F.S.A., Scot., London
MACKENZIE, Dr F. M., Inverness
MACKENZIE, J. A., Esq., Burgh Surveyor, Inverness
MACKENZIE, JOHN WHITEFOORD, Esq. of Lochwards, W.S.
MACKENZIE, Sir KENNETH S., of Gairloch, Bart.
MACKENZIE, MALCOLM, Esq., London
MACKENZIE, RODERICK, Esq., London.
MACKENZIE, WILLIAM, Esq., *Free Press* Office, Inverness
MACKENZIE, WILLIAM, Esq., Merchant, Inverness
MACKINTOSH, HUGH, Esq., Merchant, Inverness
MACLACHLAN & STEWART, Messrs, Edinburgh—(2 copies)
MACLEAN, RODK., Esq., Factor for Lochalsh and Ardross
MACLELLAN, ALASTAIR MACDONALD, Esq., Munlochy.
MACRAE, A. M. M., Esq., Glenoze, Skye
MACRAE, DUNCAN, Esq., Ardintoul, Lochalsh

LIST OF SUBSCRIBERS.

MACRITCHIE, ANDREW, Esq., Solicitor, Inverness
MACTAVISH, ALEX., Esq., Merchant, Inverness
MASSON, Rev. DONALD, M.A., M.D., Edinburgh—(2 copies)
MATHESON, Sir ALEXANDER, of Lochalsh, Bart.—(10 copies)
MATHESON, ALEX., Esq., W.S., Edinburgh
MATHESON, Rev. ALEX., Glenshiel—(3 copies)
MATHESON, Colonel J., C.B., Bengal Staff Corps, Torquay—(5 copies)
MATHESON, Dr F., London
MATHESON, DONALD FRASER, Esq., London
MATHESON, E. H. M'K., Esq., Tain
MATHESON, G., Esq., Edinburgh
MATHESON, GEO., Esq., Glasgow
MATHESON, GILBERT, Esq., Inverness—(2 copies)
MATHESON, Mrs HUGH, Weston-super-Mare—(2 copies)
MATHESON, JOHN, Esq., Rutherglen—(4 copies)
MATHESON, JOHN L., Esq., Rosewell
MATHESON, KENNETH, Esq., yr. of Lochalsh—(10 copies)
MATHESON, KENNETH, Esq., jun,, Dunfermline
MATHESON, Lady, of the Lews—(12 copies)
MATHESON, MURDOCH, Esq., Hon. Hudson Bay Coy.—(3 copies)
MATHESON, MURDOCH, Esq., Inverness
MATHESON, RODERICK, Esq., A.R.S.M., of Lochalsh, London
MATHIESON, T. A., Esq., Glasgow
MELVEN, JAMES, Esq., Bookseller, Inverness—(6 copies)
MILLER, ANDREW. Esq. of Kincurdy
MORRISON, JAMES, Esq., Inverness
MUNRO, DAVID, Esq., Inverness
REID, DONALD, Esq., Solicitor, Inverness
ROSS, ALEX., Esq., F.S.A., Scot., Architect, Inverness
ROSS, JAMES, Esq., Solicitor, Inverness
SCOTT, RODERICK, Esq., Solicitor, Inverness
SHAW, Sheriff, Inverness
SHEARER, Dr, Huntly
SIMPSON, ALEX., Esq., Ex-Provost of Inverness
SMART, P. H., Esq., Art Teacher, Inverness
STODART, R. R., Esq., Lyon Office, Edinburgh
STUART, Councillor W. G., Inverness
STUART & STUART, Messrs, W.S., Edinburgh
SUTHERLAND-WALKER, EVAN C., Esq. of Skibo
SUTHERLAND, GEORGE MILLER, Esq., F.S.A., Scot., Wick

THE MATHESONS.

THE antiquity of this clan has given rise to considerable speculation among antiquarians and the family Seanachies, but, as in the case of previous clan histories, it is not our intention to go into these pre-historic mists at any length here. Scarcely any notice of the Mathesons is to be found in the public records, and in the following account of the family we shall have to draw largely upon two family MSS., copies of which we are fortunate to possess.

After some preliminary observations, the author of the "Iomaire" MS. refers to the early origin of the family in the following terms:—" Whether the Mathesons emigrated from Denmark to Scotland before they went to Ireland, and from thence to Scotland, we know not, but certain it is that they are an old race in Ireland. In Ossian's Poems mention is made of a Calmar MacMahon, an Irish chieftain who assisted Fingal in one of his wars in Ireland. It is well known that Ossian, the aged Scottish bard, flourished between the third and fourth centuries of the Christian era, so that the time when his father Fingal fought his battles, in the vigour of youth, must have been a number of years previous to that period. The name MacMathan, Mahon, or Mahony, is still prevalent in Ireland. There is a tribe of this clan in Altona and its vicinity, a town of Lower Saxony, who have written records of their descent for 500 years back or upwards. On the borders of England, and in the south of Scotland, they are called Mahons (with the omission of the Irish Mac) and Maddisons. In the peninsula of Kintyre, which is contiguous to Ireland, the ancient inhabitants were MacKiachans, MacKays, MacMaths. Such a diversity in the name for a long period is a very strong proof of the antiquity of the original tribe which emigrated from the continent. A diversity is also observed in the spelling of the Englified name, for it is written Matheson, Mathison, Mathieson, and Mathewson, and some write Mathews, omitting the termination *on*. When Kenneth, the third King of

Scotland (*alias* Kenneth MacAlpin), was at war with the Picts in the ninth century, one of the House of Monaghan, a MacMathan came to his assistance. After the termination of the war, which almost totally extirpated the race of the Picts, the King of Scotland rewarded his followers and allies with gifts of lands. In this distribution Lochalsh was bestowed on MacMathon.* His successors cannot be traced till the twelfth century. At that time flourished one of his descendants, viz., Kenneth Matheson of Lochalsh, whose daughter was married to Colin Fitzgerald, son of the Earl of Desmond."

The writer then gives the now exploded tradition, relating how this mythical Colin Fitzgerald fought with the Scottish King at the battle of Largs in 1263, and as a reward for his services obtained the lands of Kintail and the castle of Islandonain. According to this account, Matheson gave Colin a portion of Lochalsh as his daughter's portion, "on condition that he would call his first son Kenneth. This promise he violated, and named his first son Colin, but called his second son Kenneth. The Mathesons were highly offended at this violation of the marriage contract, and from that instant meditated to revenge the supposed

---

* We have express authority for the death of Bishop Duncan, the Abbot of Iona, in 1099, and that he was a son of Mœnach or Maitheanach, equivalent to MacMahon; while local tradition intimates that Kenneth II. (McAilpean), after the conquest of the Picts in the beginning of the 9th century, during a survey of his dominions, invested the MacMathon of his day in the territory of Lochailsh, which has ever since continued his Aite-Suidhe, or the provincial seat of the name, and where, thus removed from the vicinity of the Royal residence, he and his successors would have been involved in petty feuds with his restless neighbours, the account of which, with their genealogic succession, is lost in barbarous obscurity. There is a legend preserved among the clan that after the fall of Macbeth, in 1506, during a circuit of Malcolm Ceann Mor, while he held his court at Inverlochy, an individual presented himself; and on being questioned by the monarch as to his name and suit, replied that he was the chieftain of a race respectable "in days of yore," but, now left unprotected, he was wasted and oppressed by the Danes and Pirates from the adjacent isles. If there be any truth in this tradition, it probably alluded to the death of Macbeth, who as Righ of the Torpachy of Northern Ard-Ghaidheal, was really his natural protector. The sequel is that Malcolm took him under his own guardianship, and MacMahon, in reference to the terms of his reply, which he conceived militated in his favour with the king, assumed for his Brosnachadh cath, or war cry, *de guerre*, the adverb, "O Chian," or Of Yore. —*Bennetsfield MS.* The Maynes of Powis, in Clackmannanshire, the Mayns of Auchterhouse, in Forfarshire, of Lochwood in Clydesdale, of Pile in Stirlingshire, as also the Mains, are said to be descended from Magnus, the reputed ancestor of the Mathesons, as well as those mentioned in the text.

affront. When young Colin grew up, he went to visit his friends in Lochalsh, who, instead of giving an agreeable entertainment, conveyed him to a private valley in the Braes of Balmacarra, and there put him to death. The hollow where this horrid deed was perpetrated still retains the name of 'Glaic Chailean,' or Colin's Valley. . . . . The murderers fled to the north, and took refuge either in Caithness or Sutherland, where a respectable tribe of the clan is still to be found."

The author of the Bennetsfield MS., after a lengthy, learned dissertation on the origin of the tribe, and the meaning of the name Matheson, brings us down to "MacMathon of Lochailsh, Kenneth Gruamach, who is said to have married a sister of Farquhar O'Beothlain, or Mac an t-Sagairt, in the reign of Alexander II., which commenced in 1214, and by whom he appears to have been established in the constabulary of the fortress of Eilean Donan. By his lady he appears to have had a daughter, Muire or Mary, as handed down by the probable tradition of Gaelic songs; while to this day is pointed out the adjusted stone called 'Clach na Baintighearna,' or the Lady's Stone, whence Muire Mac-Mathon was in the habit of mounting her palfrey. As it stands at a place called Ard-darach, it would seem to indicate the site of Kenneth's residence in Lochailsh." The writer then describes the alleged murder of young Colin Fitzgerald in slightly different terms to our first quoted authority, and with more circumstantial detail. The offence given to the Mathesons by naming the eldest son of Fitzgerald Colin "could only be expiated by the blood of the unconscious object of [their] savage jealousy. The nurse selected for the child was unfortunately of his mother's tribe, among which she had a kindred suitor, by whom she was induced by treachery or connivance to abduct young Cailean to a retired spot called 'Glaic Chailein,' or the place of Colin's seizure; indicating that he was seized for the purpose of being done away with, and the horrid deed is said to have been perpetrated in the neighbourhood of that spot still retaining the name of 'Tor an t-Sladraidh,' or the bush [? mound] of the murdering place, or where he was put to death." He then describes how the perpetrators of the crime fled to Sutherlandshire, and became the progenitors of the Mathesons of Shiness, of whom in their proper place.

For the next two hundred years we know nothing whatever of the Mathesons, but in 1427 the "Mak Makan," who appeared before the king at Inverness, and described by Fordun as a leader of 1000 men, is claimed as the then chief of the Mathesons. The author of the Bennetsfield MS. attempts to prove that the "Alexander McRuari de Garmoran," named by Fordun as a leader of 2000 men, is the same as the chief called "Mak Makan." On this point he writes:—"We have every authority that tradition can give us for the identity of Alastair Mac-Ruari with the personage he (Fordun) calls Mak Makan, or MacMathon, as it was formerly written; and certain it is that there is no passage in clan history more familiar than this is—in the district where the MacMathons predominate—that their chief in the beginning of the fifteenth century and during the broils of Donald of the Isles was Alastair MacRuari. . . . . The MSS. tradition in our possession narrates that Alastair was married to a daughter of the Laird of MacIntosh, and the chronicles of the Earls of Ross expressly state that at that time MacMaken, or Mathon of Lochailsh, a leader of a thousand men, was chief of the clan." Gregory correctly states that the Alastair MacRuari, "leader of *two* thousand men," was Alexander MacGorrie, son of Godfrey of Garmoran, who is said by Hugh Macdonald, the Sleat historian, to have had a son "Allaster." Gregory, however, refers to "Mak Maken"; that is, he says, "MacMahon or Mathewson of Lochalsh," as a leader of *a thousand* men. This agrees with the chronicles of the Earls of Ross quoted, as above, in the Bennetsfield MS., and there is little doubt that they were two different persons, though it is likely enough Matheson's patronymic may at the same time have been "Alastair MacRuari;" and to have been leader of even one thousand men in the beginning of the fifteenth century is quite sufficient to show that he must have been a powerful Highland chief, at a time when his neighbour, Mackenzie of Kintail, had not a single namesake of his own in the whole district. Matheson or MacMakan was taken prisoner to Edinburgh on that occasion, and beheaded shortly after on the Castle Hill.

Skene holds that the MacMathans or Mathesons are represented in the manuscript of 1450 as a branch of the Mackenzies, and that their origin is deduced in that document from Mathan or

Mathew, a son of Kenneth, from whom the Mackenzies themselves take their name.* Their genealogy is thus given :—
"Muireachach mc Doincaig ic Donch ic Donch ic Muircachach mc Cainig ic Matgamna ic Cainig," that is, "Murdoch son of Duncan son of Duncan son of Duncan, son of Murdoch son of Kenneth, son of Kenneth," the last named, according to this authority, being the common ancestor of the Mathesons and the Mackenzies, his ancestor being " Aengusa ic Cristin ic Agam mc Gillaeon oig ic Gilleon na haird " ("Angus son of Christian son of Adam son of Gilleoin Og son of Gilleoin of the Aird"). In a note Dr Skene adds that " Kermac [Kenach] MacMaghan of the Earldom of Ross is mentioned in the public accounts of Lawrence le Grant, Sheriff of Inverness (then comprehending that Earldom) cir. 1263, in the reign of Alexander the Third."† The same author in his " Highlanders of Scotland" continues :—" This origin is strongly corroborated by tradition, which has always asserted the existence of a close intimacy and connection between these two clans. The genealogy contained in the manuscript is also confirmed by the fact that the Norse account of Haco's expedition mentions that the Earl of Ross, in his incursions among the Isles, which led to that expedition, was accompanied by Kiarnakr son of *Makamals*, while at that very period in the genealogy of the manuscript occur the names of *Kenneth* and *Matgamna* or Mathew, of which the Norse names are evidently a corruption." This view is corroborated by the best authorities ; and whether the Mathesons are descended from the Mackenzies or not, we have no doubt that both are descended from the Old Earls of Ross.

Another authority, with the concurrence, it is understood, of the leading Mathesons of our own time, gives the following account of the origin and early history of their ancestors :—The Mathesons derive their name from the ancestor and founder of the clan, whose name, in ancient Gaelic, is spelt Mathgamna, in more modern Gaelic Mathan, but pronounced Mahan. This name, which signifies originally a bear, has been usually considered equivalent to the English name Mathew, and has always been so translated ; and the clan, termed in Gaelic Clann Mhic

* Highlanders of Scotland, vol. ii., p. 242.
† Collectanea de Rebus Albanicis, p. 62.

Mathgamna, or Clan Mathan, have always called themselves Mathewsons, or Mathesons; that is, descendants of Mathgamna, Mathan, or Mathew. Their earliest possessions lay in the western part of the modern county of Ross, and included Lochalsh, Lochcarron, and part of Kintail, originally forming a part of the ancient province of Earr-a-Ghaël, or Argyll, granted for the first time to the Earls of Ross by Alexander II. after his conquest of Argyll in 1228; and as the Mathesons are derived by ancient genealogists from the same stock as the Earls of Ross, and their ancestor, Mathgamna, must have flourished, according to these genealogies, about this period, while his son, according to the same authority, actually appears on record in the subsequent reign as a man of power and influence in the western part of the county of Ross, it seems probable that these districts were granted by the Earl of Ross to the founder of the clan soon after he acquired possession of them. He is mentioned both in the Norse account of the expedition of the King of Norway against Scotland in 1263, and in the Chamberlain's Rolls for that year in connection with that expedition. In the former it is said that in the summer of 1263 "there came letters from the Kings of the Hebrides, in the Western Isles. They complained much of the hostilities the Earl of Ross, Kiarnach the son of Makanal, and the Scots, committed in the Hebrides, when they went on to Skye. In these Norse names, Kiarnach son of Makanal," our authority agrees with Skene that "it is not difficult to recognise, Kenneth son of Mathgamna. The notice in the Chamberlain's Rolls for 1263 is in these terms:—Item, Kermac MacMaghan, C.S., pro vigintio vacc, de fine comitis de Ross dat. eidem per comitem de Buchan et Alanum Hostiarium habentes protestatem dni. regis per literas suas patentes tempore aduentis regis Norwagie."*
According to the same authority, the chief crime for which Matheson had to appear before James I. at Inverness in 1427 was the part he took in the sanguinary battle of Drumnacoub, in Sutherlandshire. He was, however, soon liberated, but was afterwards killed by the Mackays, with four of his sons, for the death of their chief by Matheson at that battle. This is scarcely consistent with Sir Robert Gordon's account of that engage-

---

* Lineage of the Matheson Family, in the supplementary volume of Burke's "Dictionary of the Landed Gentry," 1848.

ment, who makes no mention whatever of Matheson or any other of the Western chiefs in his description of the battle.

During his rule a dispute arose between him and the House of Sutherland out of the following curious circumstance. Matheson had a celebrated deer-hound named "Broddam Glas." Sutherland asked for a loan of the hound, which Matheson at once granted him, but the dog could never be got to stop anywhere. It always found its way back to Lochalsh from any part of the Highlands. The dog soon returned from Sutherland, and his Lordship again sent for him, but Matheson replied that "while the Earl had been quite welcome to the use of the dog for a time, he was not disposed to have him altogether alienated from himself to any man." The result was an invasion by the Earl and his followers of the Matheson country, and a desperate conflict ensued, in which the invaders were defeated and their leader killed.

The author of the "Iomaire" MS. gives the following interesting details. Lord Sutherland was so irritated at Matheson's reply, "that he raised an army to invade Matheson's property. Thereupon he took the Hill road westward, till he came to Lub-a-Ghoill. As soon as Matheson heard of his arrival he collected all his men to oppose him. There is a particular spot, at Acha-na-hinich of Lochalsh, called 'Dail Acha-da-thearnaidh' (that is, the field between the two descents), where the Mathesons were wont to assemble when going out to battle, thinking it lucky to set off from that place on any expedition. From this station Matheson marched up through Glen Uddalan, till he came in sight of the Sutherlands, who were encamped on a hill in the Braes of 'Poll-an-Tairbh,' which hill bears the name of 'Cnoc-nan-Cattach' to this day. Matheson kept himself concealed from the enemy till he got behind a hill opposite to them, which, from him, still retains the name of 'Cnoc Mhic Ruari.' Both parties came to an engagement on a plain between the two hills. They fought valiantly till perceiving a party sent to Matheson by his father-in-law, Mackintosh, as a reinforcement, advancing on an adjacent height, the Sutherlands betook themselves to flight. Many were killed in the retreat, and among the rest Lord Sutherland himself, who was buried near a river's side in Ault-nam-Bran of Glen-Luinge; and that spot still bears the name of 'Lub-a-Mhorair,' or the Earl's Curve. Their flight was so precipitate that, to avoid being taken, they threw their baggage in a little lake, which still goes by the name of 'Lochan-na-h-Ullaidh;' that is, the Lake of the Treasure. For this cause he was accused before the king, as a man of the worst character, apprehended, brought to Edinburgh and beheaded there. He left two sons—

1. John, his heir.
2. Donald Bàn,* from whom the Mathesons of Sutherlandshire.

But their mother having married, according to the Iomaire MS., a son of Macleod of Lewis, or, according to the Bennetsfield MS., Angus Macleod of Assynt, the boys fled; the elder to his grandfather, Mackintosh of Mackintosh, the other to Caithness. Captain Matheson of Bennetsfield goes into details, and states that "Angus Macleod of Assynt, tempted by the property committed to her trust, married the widow, as appears by the writs of the family of Geanies. Norman, second son of Torquil Macleod, 4th Baron of Lewis, obtained from his father the Barony of Assynt, and died in the reign of James I., and left a son, Angus, who succeeded him and married Margaret Matheson, heiress of Lochalsh. The Baronage (Douglas's), we perceive, involves this lady in two mistakes. In the first, Margaret, third daughter of Malcolm, 10th Laird of MacIntosh, grandson of Rory Mor Macleod of Lewis, was married to the Chief of Clan Tearlaich or Maclennan, whereas she was the widow of Alastair MacRuari. The second [mistake] was that she was heiress of Lochalsh, while she was in fact only tutrix for her son, the young Chief of MacMathon and Laird of Lochalsh; and it is notorious that Angus of Assynt failed to establish a footing there; and the mode of his expulsion is duly related. It is also inserted [in the Baronage]

---

* This young gentleman, who had fled to Caithness for shelter from his step-father, "got Lord Caithness' daughter with child. When she found herself in this condition, she escaped and went round to the West Coast, wishing to get to Lochalsh. After her arrival there she was delivered of a son at the roadside, between Erbusaig and Balmacarra. This son was called Iain Gallach (*i.e.*, John of Caithness), and the place where he was born still retains the name of 'Leachd Iain Ghallaich,' a cairn being erected on the spot to commemorate the fact. From him descended a numerous offspring, who were distinguished from the rest of the Mathesons by the term 'Clann Iain Ghallaich.' Of these are Alexander Matheson in Arincachdaig, and Duncan his brother; Roderick Matheson in Port-a-Chuillean; and others in Skye."—*Iomaire MS.*

that a nameless daughter of MacIntosh was married to a Macleod in the reign of James I., but the account we have received reconciles all discrepancies." The property of Lochalsh was no doubt usurped by Macleod during the minority of the heir, and we shall now proceed to show how he was finally driven out of the district by the rightful heir, and to describe the means which he adopted to attain his object and secure the ancient patrimony of his house for himself and for his successors. In doing this we shall draw freely upon the best portions of the two MSS. already quoted.

The immediate consequence of the marriage of Angus Macleod of Assynt to Matheson's widow was the flight of the heir of Matheson to his grandfather, Mackintosh, and of the younger son to Caithness. For a time the family patrimony continued usurped until John, arriving at manhood, solicited the aid of Mackintosh in the recovery of the possessions of his ancestors. This was at once promised by his grandfather, and John immediately communicated his intentions to his trusty friends in Lochalsh, all of whom entered cordially into his plan of operations.

Macleod, who all along feared that the heir might return and be loyally received by the natives, placed spies throughout the district to inform him of any danger that might occur. It was then the custom for a certain class of beggars—outcasts from their respective tribes—to seek shelter among other clans, which was usually, according to the prevailing custom of the times, accorded to them. They were known among the natives as "Buthanaich," (literally, livers in tents), and they were usually ready to perform any task, however degraded, which was allotted to them by those who sheltered them.* One of these, says the author of the Bennetsfield MS., was on this occasion insinuated by Macleod into every family. "Aware of this, it was concerted that on their retiring to rest, these noxious parasites should be severally despatched" on the night Matheson should introduce his body of resolute volunteers from Mackintosh. On his arrival with these, he formed his little band in a hollow between Reraig and Kirkton of Lochalsh, at a place called to this day "Glac nam Fear," and he then proceeded alone, disguised as a hawker of wool, and carrying a wallet of fog or heath, to "Torr-an-t-Slachdaire," where

* According to the "Iomaire" MS., these were "some of his own (Macleod's) countrymen, whom he thought well affected towards him."

Macleod and his wife resided. He sent a message to the lady, asking if she would purchase any of his fancy wools, when she requested him to come in and submit samples of what he had along with him. While exhibiting his varieties, he managed to introduce a reference to her eldest son, and artfully contrived to ascertain whether she wished to see him some day reinstated in his ancestral possessions. Discovering that she entertained friendly feelings for him, he at once made himself and his designs known to her, and he was warmly received. During the night all the Buthanaich were slain in accordance with the pre-arranged plan, except one named MacEachern, who managed for some time to escape capture, but was finally overtaken and slain as he arrived within a short distance of Macleod's house, whither he was proceeding to inform him of what had occurred; and the place where he was slain is still called "Featha Mhic Eachern," or MacEachern's Fen. Meantime young Matheson had surrounded the mansion-house and set it on fire, "he himself attending to the safe escape of his mother, which she effected; but not before she had secured that of her husband, concealed under her nightgown, and who, after she had passed those placed to intercept him, reached 'Doirre Damh,' in Duirinish, where he engaged a poor boatman to convey him to Lewis, under promise to give him a free grant of land. On his arrival, however, the Laird of Macleod, indignant at what had happened, ordered a gallows to be erected by the oars of the boat, and, hanging up the Lochalshman, observed sarcastically, that at the foot of the gallows he might enjoy free land for ever in terms of Angus' promise." Soon after Macleod attempted a descent on Lochalsh, landed at Ardhill, and came to an engagement at Kirkton, where he was again beaten at (a place still called) "Blar-nan-Saighdearan," and his retreat having been intercepted,* a number of the routed

* A party of Matheson's men stood between them and the shore to prevent their embarkation. These were headed by a Matheson of the name of Iain Ciar Mac Mhurchaidh Mhic Thomais, who made great havoc among the enemy with his arrows. Part of his descendants are dispersed between the parishes of Urray and Redcastle, of whom I shall mention particularly Alexander Mackenzie, late agent for the British Linen Company, Inverness, and Francis Mackenzie, merchant, Kyleakin. Both their grandfathers changed their original names, viz., Thomas Bain in Redcastle, and Murdoch Bain, his brother, in Brahan. There is a gravestone in the Churchyard of Lochalsh having the effigy of a *dead corpse* [sic] cut upon it, which the said Iain Ciar quarried and carried down on his back from the Braes of Kirkton.—*Iomaire M.S.*

force threw themselves into the church, trusting to it, as a sanctuary usually observed in those days. The sacrilege was, however, disregarded in this instance by one Duncan Matheson, who set fire to the building, and hence, ever after, retained the sobriquet of "Donnachadh-an-Teampuill;" and whose trespass, notwithstanding, did not incur the penalty through many generations of descendants, as two of them became highly respected clergymen of the Established Church, and another a celebrated local Bard.* Meantime Macleod himself, with a remnant of his broken followers, escaped, but was not so fortunate in a subsequent expedition, for, soon after, having landed at Fernaig, he was encountered by Matheson at Sail Fearna, again overpowered, and killed.

On the death of Sir Dugald Mackenzie John Matheson married his widow, and succeeded him as Constable of Islandonain Castle, in the defence of which he was killed by the Macdonalds under their chief, Donald Gorm in 1539. By his wife he had one son named after the priest, Sir Dugald Mackenzie, by whom he was succeeded in about one-third of Lochalsh. He was known among the Highlanders as

DUGALD ROY MATHESON. The other two-thirds of the ancient patrimony of the family had been acquired by Mackenzie of Kintail and Macdonald of Glengarry. [See Histories of the Mackenzies and the Macdonalds.]

The rent was in those days collected in kind, and a dispute arose between Glengarry and Dugald Matheson, who raised the Lochalsh rents in common, about their division afterwards among themselves. The particulars of this quarrel are given in the two MSS. already named. The following version from the Bennetsfield MS. is the most complete:—"Dugald Roy still retained the patrimony of his grandfather Alastair, and Glengarry and he were in the habit of pasturing and taking their rents jointly, as these consisted merely of the produce of the country, and subject

* Mr Matheson, minister of Kilmuir, and his nearest relatives are descended of that Duncan, so was Murdoch Matheson, the bard. A tribe of Mathesons were once the principal inhabitants of Strathbran, where they had a separate burying-place for themselves, to which no other person laid claim, and where none of any other name is interred to this day. It is called Cnoc-nan-Cleireach (*i.e.*, the Hillock or Tumulus of the Clergy). From this name it may be inferred that it was a place of worship. Around the Tumulus is still visible the foundation of a circular ring of stones.—*Iomaire MS.*

to a subsequent division by their several oversmen. On one occasion, unfortunately, there happened to be an odd 'cabag' or separate piece of butter, which Macdonald's man arrogantly insisted should become the property of his master, and Matheson's as pertinaciously refusing, divided the subject of contention with his dirk or hanger; an action which, however just, on representation gave mortal offence to his irascible co-proprietor, who swore that Mac Mathon would not possess a similar opportunity by that time next year; and it appears he took an execrable mode of ensuring his own prediction. The first step was to break off with Matheson and pick a quarrel with him; and aware that he was so notoriously prejudiced against the flesh of goats, that it would be a studied insult to present it to him, Macdonald ordered a lamb to be fed on goat's milk, and under a show of hospitality invited the other to dine with him at a castle he possessed, and the ruins of which are still to be seen, in Loch Achana-hinich. So unsuspectingly was Matheson thrown off his guard by the familiar courtesy of his host that, instead of his usual retinue of twelve and his Gille Mor (for with such a guard men of his rank visited in those days), he was attended only by his Gille Mor, or champion. The first dish set on the table was of the lamb fed as above, which he no sooner tasted than, imagining it kid, he rejected it; and being sarcastically asked by his entertainer, What objection he had to the dish? he angrily replied, 'You know I do not eat goat's flesh.' Glengarry as warmly asserted that Matheson had never ate of more genuine mutton, and he as pertinaciously insisted upon its being goat. From the dispute, as had been contemplated and preconcerted, arose a quarrel; Dugald Roy was immediately overpowered, bound, and conveyed prisoner to Invergarry, where he soon after died in confinement from the effect of this indignity." He married a daughter of the Rev. John MacRa, third son of Christopher Mac-Ra, known as "Gillecriost MacDhonnachaidh,"[*] by whom he had issue—a son,

MURDOCH MATHESON, commonly called "Murchadh *Buidhe*," or Murdoch with the yellow hair. He was so indignant at his father's treatment by Glengarry that he determined to be revenged upon him at whatever cost, and to en-

[*] See History of the Macdonalds, and the "Genealogy of the MacRas."

able him to punish him effectually he proposed to enter into an arrangement with Mackenzie of Kintail, and offered to cede to him the whole of Lochalsh in return for his aid in prosecuting his vengeance against Glengarry, retaining only to himself the reversion of Fernaig and Balmacarra. Kintail, according to one authority, "readily entered into terms so advantageous to himself, and which he, in due time, found means to convert to purposes far more favourable to himself than had been contemplated" by Matheson; while another informs us that he took possession of the lands in terms of the proposed arrangement, "but neglected to perform the other part of the agreement." Murdoch left issue—

1. Roderick, who after his father's death succeeded to Fernaig.

2. Dugald, to whom his father bequeathed Balmacarra.* He had three sons, the first two of whom, Murdoch and John, were twins. The third was called Dugald Og. Murdoch was liberally educated, his father intending him for the priesthood. He, however, did not adopt the clerical profession. A misunderstanding occurred between him and Mackenzie of Kintail, "on account of some money which Mackenzie took from him by force. For this cause he went and entered a complaint before the King, who told him that 'for as soon as he could be at home his money would be there before him, and that he might have Mackenzie's head if he pleased;' at which proceeding Mackenzie was so much enraged that, slighting the King's authority, he forced Murdoch to quit Lochalsh and to take lands in Sleat. His first wife dying there, he married next a sister of Roderick Mackenzie [fourth] of Davochmaluag, by whom he had one son named Alexander. In consequence of this marriage intercession was made for him to Mackenzie, and an agreement made that he should return to Lochalsh and pay rent for Balmacarra.† Alex-

* There is a decreet for certain sums at the instance of James Cowie against "Dougall Mathewsone in Apilcroce as heir served and retoured to the deceased Murdow Mathewsone in Bellmacarra" (who was still alive on the 28th of June 1681), dated and registered "At Fortrose, 7 March 1686."—*Fragment of Deeed, Sheriff-Clerk Office, Tain.*

† Murdoch Matheson of Balmacarra appears in the Valuation Roll of the County of Ross in 1644 as heritor of lands in the parish of Lochalsh to the value of £100 Scots per annum. There is a document in the Sheriff-Clerk Office, Tain, endorsed, "Inventar, Christane Clerk, confermit 1668," and which within it is described as "Inventar of guids, &c., which pertained to the deceased Christane M'Lennan, spouse to Murdo Mathesone in Bellmackarra, within the parish of Lochalsh, who died in August 1654,

ander, his son, left but one natural son called Kenneth. That Kenneth had a son called Murdoch, who died soon after marrying, leaving a son called Dugald, who was father to Donald, the late miller in Fernaig, and his brothers."* Murdoch also left a daughter, Agnes, who married Thomas Mackenzie, first of Highfield; and another, "who married to Kenneth Og MacQueen of Troutrome, in Skye, grandfather to the late Lady Raasay." John, the other twin (whom the midwife maintained to be the first-born, but who was denuded of his birth-right by his brother Murdoch, "who suborned witnesses against him for that purpose in order that all the patrimony left them jointly might fall to his own share"), was called Ian Og, denoting him as the youngest of the two. He married a daughter of John Mackenzie, fourth of Hilton, by whom he had three sons—Alexander, from whom the MATHESONS OF ARDROSS AND LOCHALSH, and of whom hereafter; Duncan, and Dugald, both of whom left issue, who settled in Lewis, Skye, Lochalsh, Lochcarron, and in Ireland. Dugald's third son, Dugald Og, had a son, John, who had six sons— Roderick, Donald, Kenneth, Murdoch, John, and Dugald, (known as "Dugald Beg MacIan Mhic Dhughaill.") Roderick and John left issue, whose descendants lived respectively in Kirkton of Lochalsh and Plockton. Dugald Beg left female issue only.

3. A daughter, said to have married Eachainn Cam, son of Hector Roy Mackenzie, first of Gairloch.†

Murdoch was succeeded by his eldest son,

given up be the same Murdo her said husband in name of Dugall and Christane, lawful children procreate twixt Murdo and the defunct, exrs. dative to the defunct. The amount is £4666 13s, confirmed on the last day of July 1668, at Lochalsh, in presence of Colin Mackenzie of Kilcoy, commissar. In the same place there is another document, dated 1676—a summons, "Mathewson ag. Mathewson"—in which "the Sheriff states that it has been shown to him be Dugall Mathewson in Bellmacarra, only son of the first marriage of Murdow Mathewsone, his father, by the deceased Christane Clerk, his first spouse, and also executor dative decerned to his said mother deceased that by contract of marriage twixt the deceased Dugall Mathewsone, Chamberlayne of Lochalsh, for himself, and taking burden for his lawful son, the said Murdow and Mr Donald Clerk, minister of Lochalsh, and taking burden for his said umq^u daughter, of date 27 April 1631, certain sums were provided to the heirs of the marriage, which, not being paid by the said Murdow, he is desired to show cause for not doing so, on 15th February 1676.

* Iomaire MS.

† Bennetsfield MS. If this is correct she must have been a second wife. We have met with no trace of this marriage in the Gairloch Records.

RODERICK MATHESON, designated "of Fernaig." He inherited the family resentment against the house of Glengarry, and, in 1602, entered into a bond of amity with Kenneth, afterwards first Lord Mackenzie of Kintail, when the latter obtained a commission of fire and sword against Donald MacAngus of Glengarry. Matheson took a leading part in the terrible feuds which took place between the Mackenzies and the Macdonalds at this period, and signally distinguished himself at the final taking of Strome Castle from the grandson of him who treacherously inveigled and contributed to the downfall and death of Dugald Roy Matheson, his grandfather.* From this period a warm friendship was maintained between the families of Mackenzie and Matheson.

He married a daughter of Donald Mor MacIan Mhic Fhionnlaidh, described in one manuscript as "Chief of the Finlaysons in Lochalsh." By her he had issue, an only son—

JOHN MATHESON, who succeeded him in Fernaig, and known among his own countrymen as "Ian MacRuari Mhic Mhathoin." The author of the Bennetsfield manuscript, referring to the charter obtained by Mackenzie of Kintail to the whole lands of Lochalsh in 1607, says that "we have by us, as the result of a gradual recognition, receipts for rents received by Seaforth to John of Fernaig of Lochalsh, a designation still retained by his successor even after he had acquired the estates of Bennetsfield and Suddy."

John married Anne, called "Anna Bheag nam mac mora," or Little Anne with the great sons, daughter of Alexander Roy,† a natural son of John Glassich, II. of Gairloch, by whom he had issue, an only son—

---

* For a full account of these terrible feuds, see "The History of the Macdonalds and Lords of the Isles," just published, and "The History of the Mackenzies," both by the same author.

† Iomaire MS. Captain Matheson, in the Bennetsfield Manuscript, attempts to prove that John married a daughter of Rory Mackenzie, I. of Redcastle. We have no hesitation in saying that he is in error. One of Redcastle's daughters married a *Dunbar* of Bennetsfield, and Captain Matheson must have confused this Dunbar with his own ancestor, who became the purchaser of the Bennetsfield property. The relationship of the children with Alexander Roy of Gairloch will be established in the text from the fact that John was educated by Alexander Roy's grandson and his own cousin-german, the Rev. Murdoch Mackenzie, chaplain to Lord Reay's Regiment, and afterwards Bishop of Moray and Orkney in succession. This fact is recorded even by the author of the Bennetsfield Manuscript, though he disputes the marriage connection.

1. John,* who succeeded his father.

He married, secondly, a daughter of Cameron of Caillort, Lochaber, with issue—

2. Farquhar, progenitor of a family of Mathesons who settled in Glenshiel.

3. Murdoch, who lived in Achamore, and was an excellent swimmer. It is related of him that on one occasion, accompanying Mackenzie of Kintail to Lewis, he performed a remarkable feat. As they were passing the north point of Plockton, Mackenzie, who was amusing himself with his silver-hilted sword on the gunwale of the vessel, accidentally dropped it into the sea. Murdoch, noticing Mackenzie's regret for his valued blade, immediately leaped overboard, dived to the bottom, and soon appeared with what turned out to be only a tangle of sea-ware in his mouth. He soon repeated the performance, and, after a considerable search below, made his appearance this time with Mackenzie's sword between his teeth. For this service Mackenzie made him a grant of that part of Achamore called Glas-na-Muclach to himself and his heirs for ever; but having no charter for it, it was lost after the death of his son Ewen. A sunken rock near the spot where the sword was picked up is still called " Sgeir a Chlaidheamh," or the Rock of the Sword. Murdoch's descendants settled in Plockton and in Troternish, Isle of Skye.

4. Roderick, called "Ruari Beg," a celebrated swordsman, distinguished for his intrepidity and courage. He fought with Kintail in his conquest of the Lewis; and he is said to have challenged Ian Garbh Mac 'Ille Challuim of Raasay to single combat. He was invariably the leader in pursuit of the Lochaber men who on occasions paid a visit on the business of cattle-lifting

---

* The author of the Iomaire MS. makes this John the second son, and says that there was a first son, Alexander, who lived in Duirinish of Lochalsh, and from whom the author of the manuscript was descended. Indeed the author claims for himself the chiefship of the clan, and if Alexander were legitimate his contention might possibly be maintained. That the chiefship is in the Bennetsfield family, descended from John named in the text, is generally admitted by the Mathesons themselves. We adopt this view in the text; but we shall deal with the question more fully when giving an account of Alexander's descendants later on. There is no doubt whatever that John succeeded his father in Fernaig, which fact is of itself pretty conclusive evidence that he was the eldest *legitimate* son. Farquhar is not mentioned in the Iomaire MS., while neither Murdoch nor Roderick Beg, whose names are given in the text, is referred to in the Bennetsfield Manuscript.

THE MATHESONS.

to the west, and Ruari seldom failed to overtake them and recover the *creach*. He has been locally commemorated in this connection in the following lines :—

> Ruari Beag MacIan Mhic Ruari Mhic Mhurchaidh Bhuidhe,
> Dha math thig clogaide cruadhach is pic iughair,
> 'Bheireadh Creach a tir an namhaid gun aon umhail.

Roderick died without issue.

John Matheson was succeeded in Fernaig, by his eldest son, John, commonly called "Ian Mor."

JOHN MOR MATHESON, who, although he afterwards, as will be immediately seen, purchased extensive estates in the Black Isle, always continued to style himself of Fernaig, in Lochalsh. He was liberally educated under the superintendence of his relative, Murdoch Mackenzie, grandson of Alexander Roy, a natural son of John Glassich Mackenzie, second Baron of Gairloch. Murdoch, who was an Episcopalian, served as Chaplain in Lord Reay's Regiment in the Bohemian and Swedish service, under Gustavus Adolphus; and on his return home he was presented to the parishes of Contin, Inverness, and Elgin, in succession. In 1662 he was elected to the Bishopric of Moray, and subsequently, in 1677, translated to the See of Orkney.* The author of the Iomaire manuscript states that John "was taken up" by the Bishop of Moray, "who resided at Kinkell.† The Bishop kept him for some time at school, and gave him 500 merks Scots to traffic therewith. After following the mercantile line for some time, in which he was very successful, he began cattle dealing, by which he became master of a good deal of money." Starting in life under such auspices, it is not surprising to find John Mor cutting out a career for himself. His friend, the Bishop, pointed out the source of wealth which might open up to him if he could succeed in driving some of the superfluous herds of black cattle which then abounded in the Highlands to the southern markets, and which were then of scarcely any value among his own countrymen, but, on the other hand, often served as a temptation to spoliations and feuds among themselves. John Mor at once saw the force of his cousin's advice. But there were various

---

* For Murdoch's descendants, see "The History of the Mackenzies," by the same author, p. 314.

† Hence we presume the name *Bishop*-Kinkell.

obstacles in the way at that time not easily surmounted, the most formidable being the opposition and danger certain to be met with from those powerful chiefs and clans through whose territories his droves would necessarily have to pass on their way to the southern markets.

The most powerful chiefs in his course were the Marquis of Huntly and Mackintosh of Mackintosh, each of whom had extensive possessions in Lochaber, through which Matheson would have to drive his herds. These gentlemen at the time had differences among themselves, and were jealous of each other. Matheson, ascertaining this, hit upon a ruse by which he succeeded in playing off the one against the other. To each he wrote a letter under pledge of the strictest secrecy, that the other was preparing a foray to plunder his property. "Mackintosh proceeded immediately thither, and by this precaution seemed to confirm the feigned intelligence to the other. Huntly lost no time in following. John Mor, seeing his stratagem succeeded so well, he collected as many cattle and followers as he could, and forced a route through Badenoch [in Mackintosh's absence in Lochaber] to the low countries." Our authority, while expressing a doubt as to the morality of these proceedings, commends the patriotism of his ancestor for "having driven the first herd of black cattle across the Grampian hills from the North, which exhibits him as a benefactor to the wilds of his nativity; and he found ample recompense in success, insomuch that some time after his return he purchased the lands of Bennetsfield, on the Moray Firth, as a low-country grazing and shelter for his future herds. He was now joined in his traffick by Sir William Gordon of Embo, in Sutherlandshire, but was prevented from ever residing permanently on his purchase by a fastidious reluctance of his wife to conform to the mode of living on corn, then more widely adopted in the more cultivated districts, in consequence of which he purchased the place of Easter Suddy for his son in 1688; and it is to be observed that though John was long before possessed of Bennetsfield, he continued to adopt the style of Fernaig, while his son appears in the first Parliament of William and Mary, during the life of his father, as a Commissioner of the County of Ross, under that of Bennetsfield. John's continued success appears in the various large sums of money which he was able to advance to his relatives and friends. He purchased the estate of Applecross, which had been forfeited in 1715, in the person of Alexander, IVth Laird, who had joined the Earl of Mar, which he procured to be re-conveyed to Roderick Mackenzie of Kinwhillidrum, his son and heir, and who carried on the line of Applecross." Besides these John Mor granted many other extensive loans, "some of which still rank among a set of old fruitless actions at the instance of his grandson."*

While it is quite possible that John Mor Matheson may have been the first, as his representative here claims for him, who had sent cattle to the southern markets from his own particular part of the Highlands, official documents exist which show that from Argyll and other districts cattle were so sent considerably more than a century before he ever thought of starting in the business of a Highland drover.

In 1565 we come upon a complaint "on behalf of Allane Fischear, Thomas Fischear, and certane thair collegis," dealers in cattle from the West Highlands, against Patrick Houston of that Ilk, for taking the cattle from them, when "according to thair accustamat maner" they brought them from Argyll "to be sauld to thair Hienesses liegis in the lawlands," when it was ordered by the Privy Council that such parties were not to be molested, provided that they did not "transport na victualis into Ergyle" in return.† In the following year a proclamation was issued that none presume to molest the Highlanders resorting to the markets in the Lowlands. Modernised in spelling it reads:—

At Edinburgh, 17th July 1566.—Forasmuch as through the troubles occurring the last year, the inhabitants of the county of Argyle, Lorne, Breadalbane, Kintyre, and the Isles, were afraid to come into the Lowlands for fear of invasion and such other impediments as then occurred, which trouble, thanks to God, is quieted, to the honour of our sovereigns and wealth of their subjects: And since it is not only needful that good neighbourhood and abstinence from all displeasure and invasion be observed among all the lieges; but that either of them sustain and relieve each other's necessities by interchange of "the excrescence and superflew" fruits grown in the Low and High lands; so that necessarily markets must be kept, and all men, indifferently, without exception, repair thereto for selling their goods and buying again of such necessaries as are unto

* Bennetsfield MS.

† This was in consequence of the opponents of the Queen's marriage, who had taken up arms, having been obliged by the Royal forces to retire to Argyle, and a proclamation was issued, dated the 3d of November 1565, forbidding the supply of any provisions to the rebels under severe penalties.

them needful and requisite: Therefore ordains letters to be directed to officers of the Army, charging them to pass to the Market Crosses of Perth, Stirling, Dumbarton, Renfrew, Glasgow, Irvine, Ayr, and all other places needful, and there, by open proclamation, command and charge all and sundry our Sovereign Lord and Lady's lieges, that none of them take upon hand to invade or pursue others, whether they be Highlandmen or Lowland; or to offer or make provocation of trouble, or tuilzie to others, notwithstanding any offence, quarrel, or question falling in the time of the said troubles, under the pain of death: Discharging all Sheriffs, Stewards, Bailies and other Deputies and officials, and all Provosts and Bailies of Burghs, of all staying, arresting, stop trouble, or impediment-making to the said Highlandmen in bodies or goods in their coming to the said markets, remaining therein, or departing therefrom; for any crime, action, cause, or occasion, committed during the time of the said troubles, or proceeding thereon, and of their offices in that part; but that all men pursue justice by the ordinary civil manner as appertains.*

In the Bennetsfield manuscript a curious and interesting account is given of the way by which the family ultimately obtained possession of Invermaine, in Strathconan. The manner in which this property was acquired by the family of Fernaig betrays the depressed state at that period of the lately affluent and powerful Barons of Kintail. In writing to Kenneth, IIIrd Earl of Seaforth, his contemporary, Lord Tarbat, says, "his estate was overburthened to its distractione;" and his tenacious adherence to Charles II. did not tend to enhance his prospects. It was when under this pressure that John Mor Matheson, then indifferently designed of the two Fernaigs and Ach-nan-Cleireach, or of Bennetsfield, returned from one of his lucrative excursions to the south. The produce, according to the custom of the times, was in gold; and this was carefully concealed, and the place of its deposit only known to the members of his own family. Through this channel, however, the Earl of Seaforth found means of ascertaining the secret, which led him to appropriate clandestinely so expedient a succour in his extreme need. A sister, named Mary, resided under John's roof; his precautions did not escape her vigilance, and she carried information to the Earl of Seaforth which disclosed to him the place in which her brother's treasure was concealed, whereupon his Lordship carried it all away. The treachery as well as the chief actor was soon detected, and, while she was consigned to the execration of her own clan under the designation of Mairi 'n oir, or Mary of the gold, John selected a faithful band of followers with whom he marched secretly to Brahan Castle,

* Collectanea de Rebus Albanicis, pp. 151-153, where other curious documents relating to the same subject may be consulted.

then in a feeble state of defence. Arriving, he immediately walked in and found the Earl, who at once rose to salute his friend, at dinner, when John instantly declared that "he had business of some importance which must precede further ceremonial, and drawing his sword gave the astonished Earl the alternative of instant restitution of the property carried away, or instant death; showing him that his house was surrounded, and resistance or escape impossible. It was no time for deliberation, and a bond was drawn out for the amount, which was renewed by his Countess after the Earl's death, as appears by a writ of assignation, 'Siclike and forasmuch as the deceast Isobel Countess Dowager of Seafort as prin^{le}, and Kenneth Lord Marquis of Seafort, her son, as cautioner for her, by their Bond of the date the twenty-second day of June, one thousand six hundred and ninety-eight years, bound and obliged themselves and their heirs to have contented and paid John Matheson of Bennetsfield, etc., all and hail the sum of six thousand merk Scots,' in lieu of which follows an obligation to infeft and seize the said John Matheson in all and hail the town and lands of Invermaine of Glenmaine, in Strathconan, which afterwards was re-conveyed by contract of marriage to his grandson, John of Bennetsfield, and his lady, Elizabeth Mackenzie of Belmaduthy, 1730. And here for the first time, do we find the designation of John Mor exclusively restored to that of Bennetsfield; that of Fernaig as the last relic of his patrimonial territory in Lochalsh having passed into disuetude" among his successors.

In the disposition in his favour by Sir George Mackenzie of Rosehaugh, of the lands of Easter Suddy, dated 1688, he is decribed as "John Matheson of Meikle Fernaig in Lochalsh, for himself and Marie McCra his spouse, in life-rent, and Alexander, his eldest son, in fee." He was generally known among his neighbours as "An Ceannaiche Mor Fada fo Chrios," or the Big Tall Merchant, the last two words in the Gaelic indicating that he was long-legged, or long below the girdle—an article of common use and indispensibly necessary in those days to any one in the habit of carrying money or other treasure about with him on his person.

He married early in life Mary, daughter of the Rev. Donald Macrae of Dornie, minister of Kintail, by his wife Isobel, eldest daughter of Murdoch Mackenzie, V. of Hilton, with issue—

Alexander, his heir, and several daughters, one of whom, Isobel, married Kenneth Mackenzie, first of Alduinny, third son of John Mackenzie, II. of Applecross, with issue; and another, Mary, who married Donald Murchieson of Auchtertyre.

He took sides with the Chevalier and was actively engaged in forwarding his interest at the date of his own death in 1715, when he was succeeded by his only son,

ALEXANDER MATHESON, first designed of Bennetsfield, who during his father's lifetime resided at Easter Suddy as one of the partners and acting manager of his father's extensive business and estates. He married early in life a lady of the Clan Mackenzie; settled down upon his Black Isle property, and, according to the family chronicler, "resigned any pretension to the place of his nativity and seat of his forefathers," judging it "more prudent to settle among his acquired relations than to return to undefined claims, and to engage in interminable contentions under the now paramount Earl of Seaforth." He was, however, still anxious to possess a substantial Highland property, and having already the small property of Invermaine in Strathconan, he took a wadset from Alexander Mackenzie, VI. of Davochmaluag, of the lands of Lubriach and Island Mor, in the same place, as also of the Middletown of Auchnasheen, by contract dated at Wester Fairburn, on the 26th of June 1732. During the pasturing season he or some member of his family generally resided at Invermaine or at Auchnasheen.

On the advice of Alexander Mackenzie of Inchcoulter, and Sir George Mackenzie of Rosehaugh, at the time Lord Advocate for Scotland, his wife's uncles, Matheson before his father's death entered into negotiation for the purchase, jointly with his father, of the property in the neighbourhood of Bennetsfield, belonging to Sir George, for the sum of £78,011 10s 5d Scots, or about £6,500 sterling; but finding the house, yards, and parks of Pittonachty set down in the valuation at £1200 Scots, he withdrew from further negotiation. In a note of the valuation of these properties made at the time, Scatwell is entered at £36,731 16s 1d; Bennetsfield at £13,887 10s; Belmaduthy at £9,708 8s 5d; Avoch and Milne thereof at £11,630 9s 5d; and Drynie at £6,053 6s 6d—all Scots money—making a total, as already said, of £78,011 10s 5d Scots, or £6,500 1s 10d sterling.

THE MATHESONS.   23

Alexander, though very successful in his earlier years in adding to his means, latterly involved himself in difficulties by extensive advances to friends in the shape of loans, the attempted recovery of which entailed upon him in his old age, and afterwards on his posterity, interminable and expensive lawsuits, with scarcely any advantageous results. The most prominent trait in his character, it is said, "besides his prudent economy, was his liberality in the education of the children of his followers and adherents, while his writings and business habits show these were not neglected in respect to himself."

He married, in 1705, Isobel, second daughter of Roderick Mackenzie, first of Avoch, in 1671 sub-chaunter of Ross, and son of the Rev. John Mackenzie, Archdean of Ross, natural son of Sir Roderick Mackenzie of Coigeach, Tutor of Kintail, second son of Colin Càm Mackenzie, XI. of Kintail, and progenitor of the Earls of Cromarty. Roderick's wife, and Isobel's mother, was Elizabeth, eldest daughter of Simon Mackenzie of Lochslinn (fourth son of Kenneth Mackenzie, first Lord Mackenzie of Kintail), by his second wife, Agnes, daughter of William Fraser of Culbockie, relict of Alexander Mackenzie, first of Ballone, brother of Sir John Mackenzie, first of Tarbat, and son of Sir Roderick Mackenzie, Tutor of Kintail. By this lady, Isobel Mackenzie of Avoch, Bennetsfield had issue—

1. John, his heir.
2. Roderick, who died without issue.
3. Alexander, a W.S. in Edinburgh, who, in 1739, died without issue.
4. Donald, who married Margaret, daughter of John Miller of Kincurdy.
5. Kenneth, married, without issue.
6. James, who married Mary, daughter of John Macrae of Dornie (by Anne, daughter of Alexander Mackenzie, III. of Applecross, and relict of Alexander Mackenzie, II. of Kinchullidrum), with issue.

He died, far advanced in years, in 1754, when he was succeeded by his eldest son.

JOHN MATHESON of Bennetsfield, who was first taught at home by a teacher named Thomson, and to whom the father granted as his emoluments a piece of land still or lately known after him, as Thomson's Park. This teacher not only had to instruct the young laird, but any others of the youth of the district whom Alexander Matheson might select. John afterwards, with his brother Roderick, finished his education in Edinburgh, and, shortly after his return home, during his father's lifetime, he married Elizabeth, daughter of William Mackenzie, III. of Belmaduthy, when his father assigned to him, to support a separate establishment, the whole lands and fishings of Bennetsfield and Wester Half Davoch, with one-fourth of the yearly rental of Invermaine, in Strathconan.

John followed the Earl of Cromarty in 1745, in support of Prince Charles, and fought on that side, with some of his brothers, on the fatal field of Culloden. He, however, managed to effect his escape, and his experiences on that occasion and immediately afterwards are sufficiently interesting, and so minutely recorded by Captain John Matheson, late of the 78th Highlanders, last direct male representative of the family, that we are tempted to quote him at length. Referring to the loss of the last relic of their once vast possessions in Lochalsh, Fernaig, as already detailed, by Alexander, Captain John Matheson writes substantially as follows:—There now only remains for John, his (Alexander's) grandson, the tie of consanguinity and a cordial recognition by the followers of his ancestors, and their descendants of his patriarchal claims, now absolutely associated with the more modern acceptation of Scottish chieftaincy, but assimilated more expressly to those petty sovereigns of the ancient Gallic tribes. The laird, however, lived at a time when the social habits incurred by such recollections were more expensive than prudent, a fact verified by his improvident expenditure, poorly compensated to his representatives, by the vain consolation that "Jura sanguinis nunquam proscributor." He, however, took an effectual mode of risking the proscription of everything else for which he was indebted to the industry of his predecessors by taking an active part in support of the pretensions of the last of the Royal line of Stuart in concert with his kinsman, the Earl of Cromarty; and the unaccountable absence of the latter in Sutherland, where he was made prisoner, did not prevent the laird of Bennetsfield from joining Prince Charles Edward. And, notwithstanding the pressure of the House of Sutherland, which smothered many an ardent feeling towards the cause among the adherents of Lord Fortrose and other neighbours and nearest relatives, John and some of his brothers confirmed their loyalty on the eventful field of Culloden on the 16th of April 1746, which decided the dynasty which was in future to preside over the fortunes of the British Empire.

Matheson's escape was attended by several incidents of a romantic character, "which have been minutely detailed to us by his brother James, a participator and eye-witness on the occasion, a subject on which the former continued ever after to preserve a tenacious silence." The Laird had crossed the Firth on the morning of the battle in a yacht which constituted his favourite recreation; and it would appear that after the defeat of the Highlanders, he found means to secret himself in a pigstye, which, in the eagerness of pursuit, the Royalist dragoons had overlooked. Towards evening he recovered his boat, where he lay hid till darkness, which favoured his re-crossing to his own shore in Munlochy Bay, but, excited by the exertions of the day, and rendered desperate by the unlooked-for turn it took, it is not improbable that he might have had recourse to the wonted *solatium dolorosum* of those days, to account for the rash act of discharging a fusee at a small brig of war then in the offing, in the King's service, and his instantly having been brought on board the Government vessel as a prisoner, as if it would seem that his safety was in no particular to have been indebted to flight.

Here, aboard the brig, he was immediately recognised by an old friend, Mr Fraser, a clergyman of the Established Church, who, perceiving the jeopardy Bennetsfield so imprudently placed himself in, with great presence of mind stepped forward to attest his loyalty, significantly insinuating temporary aberration of mind, which suggestion, perhaps, it is fortunate, the irritated laird did not hear. The result was that Matheson was invited to join in a convivial party of Government officers, probably as much excited as himself, from opposite causes; but by their demeanour on this occasion, these gentlemen exhibited a liberal counterpart to those execrable and cowardly ruffians on shore, who, after a victory over an enemy from whom the basest of them could not withhold the tribute of chivalrous gallantry, gave the reins to indiscriminate murder and pillage; but the page of impartial history records this sickening accumulation of crime and exhibits a monument of indelible cruelty.

Matheson's accident, however, continued to befriend him. Among the ship's crew was Mr, afterwards General, Skinner, an eminent Engineer, whose business was to select a site for, and to erect a fort [now Fort-George] on the Moray Firth. With this view he enquired of Mr Fraser where the best materials were likely to be found. The latter assured the Engineer that he was fortunate in his accidental acquaintance with Bennetsfield, on whose estate was to be had the best and most conveniently situated stone quarry in the district. It was then proposed that Mr Skinner should land and make a survey on the following day. Matheson recommended landing at once, and was imperative—perhaps dreading disclosures which might prove serious. His yacht was quite ready; the Royalist was speedily embarked under the protection of the rebel chief; and on their arrival a mutual good feeling was cemented, by social habits, which was never relaxed; while it secured to the latter a semblance of loyalty which he did not deserve, and a protection which was most convenient to him at the time, and which accounts for the pertinacious silence which he ever afterwards preserved when the Rebellion of 1745 became the subject of conversation.

Long after his death an original portrait of Charles Edward was exhumed from beneath a heap of peats, where it had been concealed, in a lumber garret, in the House of Bennetsfield; and in 1838 a label, which marked the small of the butt-end of his musket, was accidently dug up by a labourer on the field of Culloden, bearing a crest and motto which he had assumed, probably in allusion to his political bias. The ancient device of the family was "O'Chian," absurdly rendered into Latin by his grandfather as "Fuimus," instead of "Per Secula." This he changed for what was more applicable to his present adventure, "Fac et Spera," with a hand dexter, bearing a scimitar, and under it "John Matheson of Bennetsfield, 10th April 1746."

This makes it appear that the musket had been made for the purpose, and accommodated to the Highlander's mode of fighting, who generally flung away his fire-arms after the first discharge, and rushed on with sword and targe, when, by the marks, the former would be recovered after the victory; and this small silver plate has, after a lapse of 92 years, betrayed a secret which our hero so unsuccessfully endeavoured to preserve.

From this period John's life was passed almost exclusively in the social enjoyment of his neighbours, or in the cultivation of a natural genius for sculpture, painting, and mechanics, with which he amused himself by turning it to the most eccentric uses. One feature of it was that of carving likenesses on walking-sticks in carricature; and this he did so well that it was not always safe to accept of an accommodation of that kind from him, without becoming liable to the risk of finding, if the borrower did not stand high in the laird's good graces, that he became supported along the road by some ludicrously severe representation of himself. These, at all events, he contrived to get into circulation, and many of his friends were thus obliged to recognise themselves to disadvantage, or quietly submit to the ridicule which his eccentricities produced.

Another faculty he possessed, connected with a beautiful style of penmanship, was that of affixing or annexing in correspondence a dash, a portrait, or perhaps the representation of an animal, or something burlesque which left no room for misinterpreting how the individual addressed or referred to stood in the opinion of the writer. It is but justice, however, to say that the sarcastic symbols were not indiscriminately indulged in; where they were used they were sanctioned by the manner of their reception. He was also remarkable for his great strength, which is attested by several existing mementoes of his personal prowess.

He was much chagrined, before his first wife's death, at the prospect of having no sons, while the reversion of his property was destined to heirs-male; and he became quite indifferent as to what became of it or his successor.

John married, first, Elizabeth, second daughter of William Mackenzie, III. of Belmaduthy (great-grandson of Alexander Mackenzie, V. of Gairloch), by Margaret, daughter of Alexander Rose of Clava,* with issue—

1. Margaret, who married Andrew Miller of Kincurdy, with issue—among others, Elizabeth, who, in 1804, married Michael Miller, and died in 1833, without issue. Michael Miller died in

---

* "History of the Mackenzies," under Gairloch Family, by the same author, pp. 352-353.

1826, and on the death of his widow in 1833, the property of Kincurdy reverted by will to her cousin, Jane Gordon, second daughter of Colin Matheson of Bennetsfield (who died in 1825). On her death, in 1849, she was succeeded in the property by Colin Matheson Milne-Miller, now of Kincurdy.

Andrew Miller died in 1809, at the age of ninety; while Margaret, his wife, died in 1811, aged eighty years.

2. Jean, who married Charles Baird, Aberdeen, with issue—among several others, Patrick, who married Miss Wedderburn, with issue—three daughters, the eldest of whom, Elizabeth, married Captain Andrew Mason, owner of a small property in Fifeshire, but who afterwards resided in Aberdeen. By her Captain Mason had two daughters, the eldest of whom, Agnes, married the late Sir Fitzroy Kelly, for many years M.P. for Ipswich, and afterwards Lord Chief Baron of the Exchequer, with issue—an only daughter, Clara. Captain Mason's second daughter, Eliza, married M. de Gerrin, a scion of an ancient family of noble descent in France.

3. Elizabeth, married William Paterson, a merchant in Aberdeen, without issue.

4. A daughter, who died unmarried.

His first wife having died in 1760, he married secondly, Christina, daughter of John Gordon, second son of Gordon of Letterfurie, by Jean, daughter and heiress of John Gordon of Achimeath, a cadet of the Gordons of Buckie. By this lady Matheson had issue—

5. Colin, his heir.

6. John, who served for several years in a Regiment of Highland Infantry, raised by the Duke of Gordon during the American War of Independence, and afterwards continued his military career in the H.E.I.C. Service, where he was appointed Military Auditor-General on the Bombay Establishment, and subsequently Paymaster to a Brigade of the Army under Lord Lake, in which position he was suddenly cut off in 1805, "universally esteemed." The following notice of his death and services appeared in the *Bombay Gazette* in December 1805 :—" On Friday, 7th December, died here Captain John Matheson of the Hon. Company's military establishment at this Presidency, and late Paymaster of the detachment of troops stationed at Poonah. A man of great kind-

ness of heart and incorruptible integrity, who in situations of public trust was actuated by the purest sense of honour, and conducted himself with scrupulous and severe probity, and who in every relation of life deserved and enjoyed the esteem of all who knew him, and could justly appreciate the worth of an honest man. During the period of 13 years' service in India, his care, diligence, and disinterestedness had uniformly recommended him to his superiors; his warm and honest heart rendered him the object of the friendship of his companions, and his great mildness, good temper, and readiness to oblige, secured the good opinion of all those who had official intercourse with him. The general feelings of this society was manifested by the unusual number and respectability of the gentlemen who attended his remains to the place of interment, among whom were most of the principal officers of the Army and several of the principal members of the Civil Department." Captain John died unmarried.

7. Catharine, who married Alexander Gillies, London, with issue, one son, Alexander, a merchant in Berbice.

8. Maria, who died unmarried.

John died at Bennetsfield House, on the 21st of February 1768, and was buried in the family burying-ground at Suddy, when he was succeeded by his eldest son,

COLIN MATHESON of Bennetsfield, then in his fifth year. The management of the property, as well as the care of the children, devolved upon the young widowed mother, whose active mind and business habits were ably assisted by the judicious counsel of her father, early trained to the law; and it can be easily believed that such qualifications as both possessed were in urgent request during a long minority while the property was heavily encumbered, its boundaries undefined and at the same time a question of dispute with the neighbouring proprietors. Indeed matters had got into such an embarrassed position that it required the greatest prudence and the most judicious exertion to preserve the property to the family.

Colin was sent to be educated, first to Elgin, where his mother accompanied him; but finding the heir's presence indispensable at home, she returned to Ross-shire with him and placed him in school at Fortrose, under Mr William Smith, well known for his excellent qualities as a teacher—qualities afterwards spoken to by many of his pupils, whose subsequent successful career in various walks of life many of them attributed to his excellent mode of instruction. In due course Colin went to Aberdeen, and finally completed his education in Edinburgh.

In 1780, when only in his sixteenth year, he received a commission in the Gordon Fencibles, raised and embodied at Aberdeen by Alexander, Duke of Gordon, in 1778. Here Colin served first as Ensign and afterwards as Lieutenant, until on the conclusion of peace between Great Britain, France, Spain, and America, the corps was disbanded in 1783.

In 1784 he married Grace (a very beautiful woman, whose portrait by Smellie Watson is in the possession of the Rev. Donald Masson, M.A., M.D., Edinburgh), fourth daughter of Patrick Grant of Glenmoriston, by his wife Henrietta, daughter of James Grant of Rothiemurchus, with issue, who arrived at maturity—

1. John, his heir.

2. Patrick Grant, a Major, H.E.I.C. Horse Artillery, on the Bengal Establishment, and for many years Chief of the Commissariat Department at Delhi, where he died in 1835. His death is referred to in the obituary of the Bengal *Englishman* of January the 17th, in that year; and in the Delhi *Gazette* as follows :— " At Delhi, on Wednesday, 15th inst., Captain Patrick Grant Matheson, Commissary of Ordnance. His remains were followed to the grave by nearly all the civil and military officers of the station, and the whole of the Magazine Establishment, many of whom shed tears of sorrow to his departed worth." He married, in India, Hannah Mills Butler, daughter of James Major Orde, an officer of the Commissariat Department, with issue—(1) James Brooks Young Matheson, Colonel, H.E.I.C.S., who commanded the 11th Bengal Irregular Cavalry; raised the Benares Horse during the Indian Mutiny; took a gun at Mooltan; and received the Indian medals and clasps. He married Lousia Keane, daughter of Dr Keane, Superintending Surgeon of the Presidency of Bengal, with issue—*(a)* Ian Grant Matheson, and *(b)* Alexander Matheson Mathon Matheson, both of whom died young in India ; *(c)* ERIC GRANT MATHESON, present chief of his clan, who, born in 1865, now resides with his mother in Belgium (who on the death of her first husband, Colonel James Brooks

THE MATHESONS. 31

Young Matheson, married, secondly, M. Vans Best); and (*d*) Ailsie Grant Matheson. (2) Thomas Theophilus Metcalf, Lieutenant, 39th Regiment, who died in India in his 21st year, unmarried; (3) Colonel Ian Grant Matheson, Staff Corps, late 2d Fusiliers, medals and clasps, now residing at Torquay; (4) Susan Eleanor, who died in infancy; (5) Isabella Maria Grant, who married James Charles Claud Hamilton, of the Hamiltons of Tyrone, Major, late Bengal European Light Infantry, medals and clasps, with issue—Claud Hamilton and Seymour Ratcliffe George Annesly Hamilton; (6) Hannah Grace, who married Lieutenant-Colonel H. King, 13th Regiment, Bengal Infantry (medal and clasp), with issue—Mortimer James King.

3. Charles Mackenzie Matheson, who, after a short apprenticeship in a mercantile house in London, emigrated to the colony of Berbice, where he carried on a large and successful business for many years. He married Margaret, daughter of Simon Fraser of Kilmorack, in that colony, by his wife Maria, daughter of Colonel Barclay of New York, a cadet of the family of Urie, with issue, six sons and one daughter. Two of the sons, who still survive, are the Rev. Charles Matheson, an ex-Fellow of Oxford, now head master of the Clergy Orphan School at Canterbury, Kent; and another, Donald, a merchant in Berbice.

4. Alexander Gordon, who joined his brother Charles in Berbice, and died there, unmarried, in 1819.

5. Christina, who married W. R. Spalding, an officer in the Barrack Department at Fort-Augustus, with issue—(1) Richard, a Colonel of Marines, married with issue; (2) Colin, an officer in the Ordnance Department, New South Wales; (3) Warner, who went to Berbice; (4) Alexander; (5) Grace, who married Charles Lesack, a Lieutenant in the Royal Artillery, with issue, one son, Charles, in the Army; and (6) a daughter, who married Major Robert Chadwick.

6. Jane Gordon, proprietrix in her own right of Kincurdy, in the County of Ross, who married the Rev. Robert Milne-Miller, minister of Aboyne, in Aberdeenshire, with issue—(1) Colin Matheson Milne-Miller, present proprietor of Kincurdy, Surgeon-Major in the Army; retired in 1873. He was Assistant-Surgeon in the 80th Regiment during the Indian Mutiny. Holds medal, 1876-77. He married, in 1866, Mary Ann Phipps, with issue—

Colin Matheson, born 18th of June 1870, died in 1872; Robert Michael, born 26th of March 1874; Jane Elizabeth, Mary Louisa, Helen Christina, Grace, and Harriet Matheson. (2) Andrew Michael Miller, C.E., massacred at Cawnpore during the Indian Mutiny in 1857. (3) George Gordon, who married Elizabeth, daughter of Dr Ross, Tain, with issue—an only daughter, Jane Dora. He died on the 27th of May 1862. (4) Elizabeth Milne-Miller, who died unmarried, in the 21st year of her age, in 1849. (5) Grace, who died in infancy.

7. Elizabeth Rupert Fraser, who married Donald Charles Cameron of Barcaldine, Argyllshire, with issue—(1) Donald, (2) Alexander, and (3) Colize, all three of whom died in infancy; (4) John, who died unmarried in 1857; (5) Allan Gordon, who inherited the family estates of Barcaldine and Foxhall, and who married Mary Colebrooke, only daughter of George William Traill of Vera and Mousey, Orkney, with issue—two sons, Ewen Somerled, present heir to the Barcaldine Estates, Allan Gordon, and a daughter, Mary Colebrooke, who died in 1878. He died in 1872. (6) Donald Charles of Glenbrittle, Isle of Skye, who married Anne, daughter of Charles Shaw, W.S., late Sheriff-Substitute of Lochmaddy, with issue—two sons and two daughters; (7) Patrick Evan, who died unmarried in 1853; (8) MariaGrace, who married James Archibald Campbell of Inverawe, with issue—four sons and five daughters; (9) Elizabeth, who married Patrick, third son of Grant of Glenmoriston, with issue—two sons and four daughters; (10) Helen, who married James Murray, youngest son of Grant of Glenmoriston, with issue—four sons and three daughters.

8. Martha Fraser, who married, first, Hugh Junor of Essiquibo, with issue—(1) Colin, a merchant. She married secondly the Rev. Archibald Brown, minister of St Andrew's Church, in Demerara, with issue—(2) Hugh of Park House, Melbourne, married, with issue—Archibald Junor, Colin Matheson, William Macdonald, Hugh Mackenzie, Martha Elizabeth, Alice, Helen Grace, and Lily; (3) Grace, who married Colonel Andrew Kelso, 3d Madras Cavalry with issue—Archibald, C.E., Bombay, and Alice Martha, who married the Rev. Alfred Swainson, M.A. of Cambridge; (4) Helen Jane, who married the Rev. Donald Masson, M.A., M.D., minister of the Gaelic Church, Edinburgh,

with issue—Donald Hugh, William Muir Macdonald, Grace Isabella, Helen Margaret, Christina Amelia, Alice Isobel, Flora Macdonald, and Kate Hamilton.

9. Helen Cameron, who married the late William Bell, surgeon in the H.E.I.C.S., a fine old lady, who still survives in Inverness.

Colin of Bennetsfield died at Fortrose, in 1825, and was buried in the family tomb at Suddy, which was renovated, and a massive slab erected to his memory, by his widow and daughters. He was succeeded by his eldest son,

JOHN MATHESON of Bennetsfield, first educated at Fortrose, and afterwards at the University of Edinburgh; but having a preference for a military profession, he joined the army in 1803. He finally retired as Captain of the 78th Highlanders. He wrote the Bennetsfield Manuscript of the Mackenzies, and an account of his own ancestors, taken chiefly from the family records, and to which we are largely indebted in the preparation of this sketch. He was a learned and accomplished man, an excellent musician, and as a linguist he was proficient in several modern languages, including Turkish; as also in Latin and Greek. His knowledge of French is said to have once stood him in good stead. Being taken prisoner while serving with his regiment in Egypt, he became the bondsman of a certain scheik, who employed him, first as his gardener, and ultimately as his secretary. While exercising the functions of the latter office in the French language, he was able to communicate in English with his family, and this in due time led to his release. Captain "Jack," as his friends loved to call him, was also a writer of verses.

He married Ann, daughter of the Rev. Robert Arthur, minister of Resolis, in the County of Cromarty, and died, without issue, shortly after 1843, when he was succeeded as representative and chief of the Mathesons by his nephew,

COLONEL JAMES BROOKS YOUNG MATHESON, H.E.I.C.S., son of Major Patrick Grant Matheson, who died at Delhi, as already stated, in 1835, and grandson of Colin Matheson of Bennetsfield, who died in 1825.

Colonel James Brooks Young Matheson married, in 1857, Louisa, daughter of Dr Keane, Superintending Surgeon of the Presidency of Bengal, with issue—

1. Ian Grant, who died young, in India.
2. Alastair Grant, who died young, in India.
3. Eric Grant, born in 1865.
4. Ailsie Grant.

He died in 1866, when he was succeeded as representative of the Mathesons of Bennetsfield and chief of his clan by his eldest surviving son,

ERIC GRANT MATHESON, still a minor, residing with his mother, who married, as her second husband, Alexander Vans Best, M.D., F.R.C.S.L. of Aberdeen, who died in 1876.

THE MATHESONS OF LOCHALSH AND ARDROSS.

AN account of this family will probably derive its greatest interest from the fact that while many of our ancient Highland families are fast disappearing, mainly in consequence of the extravagance and folly of their chiefs, the Mathesons of Lochalsh have, by the opposite qualities of prudence and business habits, been raised in our own day from a position of comparative obscurity to that of influence and wealth worthy of their fifteenth century ancestors, who are alleged to have been at that period the leaders of two thousand able-bodied warriors. At this very date the head of this branch of the Mathesons would, in similar circumstances to those which existed in those days, command from his extensive estates the allegiance of a following little short of his ancestor, though a small portion of these would be of his own name. But this would have been equally true of his ancestor of 1427, who in that year appeared before King James at Inverness.

That the single exertions of one man should have succeeded in raising the fortunes of an ancient family, which had almost disappeared as possessors of the soil for centuries, is as remarkable as it is creditable to his prudence and business energy. If to the extensive properties owned by the present proprietor of Lochalsh and Ardross we add the possessions of his late relative, Sir James Matheson of the Lewis, few of the owners of old Highland properties can boast of such a heritage in possession of the representatives of any single family, though no break may have occurred in the possession or succession; while the Mathesons owe their entire modern heritage to their own personal earnings and business industry.

It must have been gratifying to themselves, as it certainly was to all good Highlanders, to see the estates of Lochalsh, Attadale, Ardross, and the Lewis, when they had to change hands from another set of Highland proprietors, coming into the possession of the representatives of the ancient stock who owned a large portion of the same lands many centuries ago. And the manner in which they have dealt with their new possessions and with the inhabitants residing upon them, have, on the whole, been most creditable, and in consonance with the laudable and patriotic feelings and ambition which made them anxious to own the original heritage of their ancestors. We shall have more to say on this subject further on, in its proper place; meanwhile we proceed to show the descent of the present family step by step from the old stock—the ancient and original Mathesons of Lochalsh.

The reader would have observed [page 15] that MURDOCH MATHESON, known as "Murchadh Buidhe," or Murdoch with the yellow hair, had a son RODERICK who succeeded his father at Fernaig, and from whom the Mathesons of Bennetsfield, already dealt with. He had also a second son, DUGALD MATHESON, to whom his father bequeathed the lands of Balmacarra. Dugald married, and had three sons, the first two of whom were twins,

1. MURDOCH, who inherited Balmacarra, and appears in the Valuation Roll of the County of Ross in 1644 as owner of lands in the parish of Lochalsh, to the value of £100 Scots per annum. He afterwards alienated these lands to Seaforth, and paid rent for them, and ultimately, in consequence of a quarrel with his superior, he was forced to leave Lochalsh, and for a time settle in Skye. After his second marriage, however, intercession was made for him by his wife's relatives, and he was allowed to return to Balmacarra as a tenant under Seaforth, again paying rent for his original patrimony. He first married Christian Maclennan, with issue—two children, Dugald, who is described as "Chamberlayne of Lochalsh," and Christian. Dugald appears to have married Christian, daughter of the Rev. Donald Clerk, minister of Lochalsh, and had issue. We have not succeeded in tracing Dugald's children by Christian Clerk, but on the 15th of February 1676, Murdoch is required by the Sheriff of Tain to show cause why he had not paid certain sums which were provided for Dugald's heirs under his first marriage contract, dated the 27th of April 1631. Murdoch married, secondly, a daughter of Alexander Mackenzie, IV. of Davochmaluag,* after which he was permitted to return to Lochalsh. By this lady Murdoch had issue—one son, Alexander (whose only issue was a natural son Kenneth), and two daughters, Agnes,

* At page 13, this lady is described as a *sister* of Roderick Mackenzie, *fourth* instead of *fifth* of Davochmaluag.

who married Thomas Mackenzie, I. of Highfield, with issue; and another who married Kenneth Og Macqueen of Toutrome in the Isle of Skye. Murdoch's legitimate male descendants appear thus to have become extinct, when Dugald's male line fell to be carried on by,

2. JOHN MATHESON, the other twin, called "Ian Og," whom, it is said, the midwife maintained to be the first-born; but Murdoch is alleged to have suborned witnesses against his claim to be the eldest of the twins, "in order that all the patrimony left them jointly might fall to his own share." John occupied lands in Lochalsh, and married the second daughter of John Mackenzie, IV. of Hilton, by his wife, Margaret, daughter of Dunbar of Inchbrock, with issue, three sons—(1) ALEXANDER, his heir, progenitor of the Mathesons of Lochalsh, Attadale, and Ardross, and of whom presently; (2) Duncan, who left three sons—John, Kenneth, and Alexander; (3) Dugald, who had issue—two sons, John and Murdoch.

3. Dugald, called "Dugald Og," who had a son, Alexander, who left six sons, many of whose descendants are still to be found in Lochalsh.

The descent of this family from MURDOCH "BUIDHE" MATHESON, the common progenitor of the two families of Bennetsfield and Lochalsh, may be briefly stated thus:—

I. DUGALD MATHESON of Balmacarra, son of Murdoch Buidhe.

II. JOHN MATHESON, the twin, second son of Dugald, and commonly called "Ian Og."

III. ALEXANDER MATHESON, his heir, who occupied the lands of Achtaytoralan in Lochalsh, and married Christina, eldest daughter of Alexander Macrae of Inverinate, "Chamberlain of Kintail," by his first wife, Margaret, daughter of Murdoch Mackenzie, II. of Redcastle, by his wife, Margaret, daughter of William Rose, XIth Baron of Kilravock.

By his wife, Alexander Matheson had issue—

1. Murdoch, who married Catherine, daughter of John Breac, son of the Rev. Farquhar Macrae, minister of Kintail, with issue—an only son, John, who married a daughter of Kenneth Matheson, by whom he had two sons, Murdoch and Kenneth, and one daughter. Murdoch, the eldest son, died unmarried. Kenneth married Anne, daughter of Roderick Mackenzie, Rissil, with

issue—an only son, John (and two daughters), who resided at Kishorn, and died, at the age of seventy-two, in 1849, without issue, when, in his person, the male line of Murdoch became extinct.

2. John, tenant of Achtaytoralan, who married Anne, daughter of John, third son of William Mackenzie, I. of Shieldag, and sixth son of John Roy Mackenzie, IV. of Gairloch, by whom he had issue, two sons—(1) John Og of Duirinish, who married Mary, daughter of Kenneth Roy Mackenzie of Alduinny, with issue—*(a)* John, who succeeded his father at Duirinish, and married Margaret, sister of Alexander Macrae (who left the Macrae Fund for King's College, Aberdeen), with issue, several sons, two only of whom arrived at maturity. John, the eldest of these, married Isabella, daughter of James Matheson, a son of Bennetsfield. John died before his father, leaving a family of seven sons (and a daughter Mary), Alexander, Kenneth, Farquhar, James, Duncan, Roderick, and Colin. Colin married Christian, daughter of William Smith, Forres, with issue—three children who died in infancy, and William, who emigrated to Columbus in the State of Georgia, where he left one son and three daughters; Alexander, who emigrated to the same place, where he married and still survives, with a family of three sons and three daughters; Duncan, the distinguished Missionary to the Highland Brigade, during the Crimean War, and whose Memoir, by the Rev. John Macpherson, entitled "Duncan Matheson, the Scottish Evangelist," has made him so widely known, married Mary Milne Faversham, Kent, with issue—three sons and three daughters; Jessie, Colin's only daughter, married Donald Shearer, M.A., Ph.Dr., now of Huntly, without issue. Donald, the youngest son of John of Duirinish, joined the army, where he died, leaving two sons, Murdoch and Colin; *(b)* Farquhar, who went to America with his family in 1774; (2) Kenneth, who died young, unmarried; (3) Flora, who married, and became the mother of Alexander Matheson, Rector of the High School of Edinburgh; (4) another daughter.

John of Achtaytoralan married, secondly, Marion, daughter of the Rev. Finlay Macrae, minister of Lochalsh, with issue—(5) Alexander, schoolmaster at Dornie, Lochalsh, who married Catharine, daughter of James Matheson, son of Alexander Matheson of Bennetsfield, with issue, several sons, one of whom,

Farquhar Bàn Matheson, for many years Inspector of Poor in Kintail, married Isabella, daughter of Kenneth Roy Mackenzie, Kishorn, of the family of Alduinny, cadets of Applecross, with issue, five sons and two daughters. One of the sons is the well-known Highlander, Dr Farquhar Matheson, of Soho Square, London. Alexander, the schoolmaster, had also several daughters, and many of his descendants are still to be found in their native district. (6) Colin, who was liberally educated at the University of St Andrews, after which he entered the army, since which nothing has been heard of him.

3. Farquhar, direct male ancestor of Alexander Matheson of Lochalsh and Ardross, M.P., and his family, of whom presently.

4. Dugald, who was killed at the battle of Glenshiel in 1718, married a daughter of John Mackenzie, and sister of Kenneth Mackenzie, in Culdrein, Attadale, with issue—two sons and four daughters. The sons were—(1) John, who married a woman in the Isle of Skye, and died early, without issue; (2) Roderick, who married Christian Mackenzie, lived at Kishorn, and had two sons, John and Dugald, and three daughters. Roderick's descendants now reside at Perth, Ontario, Canada. John, who married Florence Macrae, and went south with his family of sons and daughters, one of whom was the Hon. Roderick Matheson, who subsequently made his mark as a Canadian politician, and became a member of the Legislative Council. Dugald was forester at Reraig, Lochcarron.

5. Donald, who married Isabella, daughter of Alexander Macrae, Conchra, Lochalsh, with issue—(1) Donald Og, who left several daughters, but no male issue; (2) John, died a young man, leaving issue, an only son, also named John, who died young, with issue, one son and two daughters; (3) Dugald, who left four sons, all of whom were alive in 1824, Alexander, John (a catechist in Sallachy, Lochalsh), Murdoch, and Duncan.

6. Colin, a merchant in Dingwall, who died without male issue, but left two daughters, the eldest of whom, Janet, married John Macneil, a builder in Dingwall, to whom she carried her father's property. The other married Roderick Maclennan, miller at Millbank, with issue, Colin Maclennan, afterwards innkeeper, Dingwall.

We shall now revert to Alexander's third son,

IV. Farquhar Matheson, designated of Fernaig, and to whom his father appears to have left most of his property. In 1687 he succeeded his cousin, John Mor Matheson of Bennetsfield, in the old family holding at Fernaig, while at the same time he held a wadset of the lands of Lussag, Kyleakin, Glenbeiste, and others in Skye, for which he paid 3000 merks Scots. "He was an active thrifty man, being generally engaged in droving and cattle dealing."*

He married, first, a daughter of Evander Murchieson of Auchtertyre, without issue. She only lived about a year after marriage. He married, secondly, his cousin Mary, daughter of Christopher Macrae, Ardintoul, grand-daughter of Alexander Macrae of Inverinate, by his second wife, Mary, daughter of Alexander Mackenzie, IV. of Davochmaluag, by his wife, Margaret, daughter of Hector Munro of Fowlis, by Anne, daughter of Hugh, seventh Lord Lovat. By this lady, Farquhar Matheson had issue—

1. John, his heir.

2. Alexander, tenant of Achandarrach, who married Mary, daughter of Murdoch Mackenzie of Sand, Gairloch, with issue—three sons and two daughters, Farquhar, Roderick, Murdoch Bàn, Catherine, and Margaret.

3. Ewen, who died young, unmarried.

4. Donald, Balmacarra, who married, first, Margaret, daughter of Roderick Mackenzie, II. of Sanachan, with issue—(1) Kenneth, who had a son, Kenneth Roy, who lived in Plockton; and (2) Roderick, educated at King's College, Aberdeen, who afterwards joined the army, and was never since heard of. He had also five daughters by this marriage, one of whom, Mary, married Donald Kennedy, Kishorn, with issue—the Rev. John Kennedy, minister of Redcastle; the Rev. Neil Kennedy, minister of Loggie; and Alexander Kennedy, farmer, Kishorn, with issue—Neil and Donald Kennedy, now residing there, and others. Catherine, the second daughter, married Roderick Mackenzie, Slumbay, Lochcarron, while the other three married and emigrated to America. Donald married, secondly, Anne, daughter of John Matheson, Duirinish, with issue, five sons—John, Alexander (the

---

* Iomaire Manuscript.

blind fiddler), Donald of Achandarrach, Murdoch, and Farquhar. He had also two daughters by the second marriage.

5, Mary; 6, Catherine; 7, Marion; 8, Anne; 9, Christian.

Farquhar died, about 1725, on his way from the Michaelmas market at Inverbenchran, Strathconan, and was buried in the church of Lochalsh, when he was succeeded by his eldest son.

V. JOHN MATHESON, who purchased for his eldest son the estate of Attadale and Corrychruby, about 1730, from Alexander Mackenzie, VIII. of Davochmaluag. He was factor for the Seaforth estates of Kintail, Lochalsh, and Lochcarron, and "was accounted the most reputable farmer in the North Highlands of Scotland."*

He married, first, a daughter of Mackenzie of Achilty, " in the Island of Lewis," with issue—two sons, who died in infancy.

He married, secondly, on the 9th of September 1728, Margaret, daughter of Kenneth Mackenzie, I. of Pitlundie, son of Alexander Mackenzie, II. of Belmaduthy, by his wife, Catherine, daughter of Sir Kenneth Mackenzie, I. of Coul, Baronet. Margaret's mother was Anne, daughter of Hector Mackenzie of Bishop-Kinkell, and grand-daughter of Kenneth Mackenzie, VI. of Gairloch. By this lady Matheson had issue—

1. Donald, his heir.

2. Kenneth, killed at the capture of Quebec, under General Wolfe, without issue.

3. Alexander, who succeeded his brother Donald at Fernaig and Attadale.

4. William, who died unmarried.

5. Farquhar, of Court Hill, who married, first, Elizabeth, daughter of William Mackenzie of Strathgarve, with issue—(1) William, a Captain in the 78th Highlanders, who died without issue; (2) Janet, who married Alexander Matheson, and emigrated to America. Farquhar married, secondly, Margaret, daughter of John Mackenzie of Achiltie and Kinellan, a grandson of Sir Colin Mackenzie, Bart., IV. of Coul, with issue; (3) an only son, Farquhar, now living in London.

6. Anne, who married Alexander Mackenzie, Kishorn, son of Captain John, fourth son of John Mackenzie, II. of Applecross.

* Iomaire Manuscript.

THE MATHESONS.

7. Mary, who married Simon Mackenzie, III. of Alduinny, with issue.

8. Catharine, who married Archibald Chisholm, grandfather of the present James Sutherland Chisholm of Chisholm.

John Matheson married, thirdly, in 1745, Elizabeth, daughter of Simon Mackenzie, I. of Allangrange (by Isobel, daughter and co-heiress of Sir Roderick Mackenzie of Findon), with issue—one son,

9. John, who married, with issue—an only son, Alexander, Captain, 78th Highlanders, who died in India, in 1809, without issue.

He died in 1760, when he was succeeded by his eldest son,

VI. DONALD MATHESON, second of Attadale, who built the mansion-house there during his father's lifetime, in 1755, and married Elizabeth, daughter of James Mackenzie, III. of Highfield (by Mary, daughter of Roderick Mackenzie, IV. of Applecross, by his wife, Anne, daughter of Alastair Dubh Macdonell, XI. of Glengarry, by his first wife, Anne, daughter of Hugh, Lord Lovat), without issue. He died in 1763. His widow married, as her second husband, Farquhar Matheson of Tullich.

He was succeeded by his brother,

VII. ALEXANDER MATHESON, third of Attadale, who, in 1763-4, married his cousin Catharine, daughter of Alexander Matheson, Achandarrach, by Mary, daughter of Murdo Mackenzie of Sand, with issue, twenty-one children, of whom only one son and four daughters arrived at maturity.

1. John, who succeeded his father.

2. Margaret, who married, as his second wife, Roderick Mackenzie of Achavannie, with issue—one son, Alexander, still living.

3. Anne, who married Farquhar Matheson of Achandarrach.

4. Mary, who died unmarried.

He died in January 1804, when he was succeeded by his only surviving son,

VIII. JOHN MATHESON, fourth of Attadale, who, in 1804, married Margaret, daughter of Captain Donald Matheson of Shiness, by Catharine, daughter of the Rev. Thomas Mackay, minister of Lairg, son of the Rev. John Mackay, by Catharine, daughter of John Mackay of Kirtomy, grand-nephew of Donald, first Lord Reay, and grandson maternally of Sir James Fraser of Brae, son of Simon, eighth Lord Lovat. By this lady, who died in 1850, Matheson had issue—

1. Alexander, his heir, now Baronet of Lochalsh, born in 1805.

2. Hugh, a merchant in Liverpool, who married, in 1837, Christina, daughter of the Rev. Alexander Macpherson, D.D., minister of Golspie, with issue—six daughters; (1) Margaret Mary Crawford, who married the Rev. Robert Cameron, D.D., Leeds, without issue; (2) Isabella; (3) Elizabeth; (4) Alexandrina Macpherson, who, on the 19th of August 1879, married Edward Foster, F.S.A. (Lond.), Aldershot, with issue—Thomas Matheson, born 3d of June 1880. Hugh's other two daughters died in infancy.

3. Farquhar, minister of Lairg, which charge he resigned in 1878. He now resides in Inverness, unmarried.

4. Donald, settled in America, where he married, with issue.

5. John, who died young.

6. Catherine, who, in 1834, married General John Macdonald, H.E.I.C.S., with surviving issue—(1) Donald, a Colonel in the Indian Army, married in April 1865, Emilia Frances, daughter of Lieutenant Crommelin, R.A., without issue; (2) John Matheson, a partner in the well-known firm of Matheson & Company, Lombard Street, London, who married, in October, 1870, Eleanora Leckie, daughter of William Leckie Ewing of Arngomery, Stirlingshire, with issue—Norman Matheson, Eric William, John Buchanan, Eleanora Leckie, Catherine Matheson, and Bertha. General Macdonald has also three daughters.

7. Harriet, who, on the 24th of March, 1835, married Charles Lyall, London, with issue—(1) Charles James, born 1845, and married, in 1870, Florence Lyall, daughter of Henry Fraser, with issue—one son and four daughters; (2) Henry, a Captain in the Royal Artillery, born 1849, and married, in 1876, Mary Sophia, eldest daughter of Colonel Akers, Royal Engineers, with issue— one daughter; (3) Caroline Alexa, who in 1865 married the Rev. Bradley Hust Alford, M.A., with issue—two daughters; (4) Harriet Jane, (5) Mary, (6) Edith Margaret, and (7) Constance.

John Matheson died in 1826, when he was succeeded, as representative of the family, by his eldest son,

IX. ALEXANDER MATHESON, now of Lochalsh, Attadale, and Ardross, M.P. for the County of Ross. During his father's lifetime the family was, in 1825, reduced to the necessity of parting with the last remnant of their heritable possessions in the west by the sale of Attadale, and Alexander Matheson had to begin life afresh without any of those advantages of position and wealth which make success in life so comparatively easy. His uncle, the late Sir James Matheson of the Lews, Baronet, was at the time largely engaged and very successful in the commercial world of India and China, and under his auspices an opening was found for young Matheson in the famous mercantile house of Jardine, Matheson, & Co., on the retirement from which he founded and became head of the eminent firm of Matheson & Company, London.

About 1839, a comparatively young man, he returned to the Highlands, where he had spent the earlier years of his life, with a magnificent fortune, and, in 1840, made his first start in the purchase of Highland property. In that year he bought the lands of Ardintoul and Letterfearn, a pretty estate of about 6000 acres, lying on the south side of Lochalsh and Loch Duich, for £15,500. In 1844 he acquired the lands of Inverinate, on the north side of Loch Duich, an ancient heritage of the Mackenzies and the Macraes, for £30,000. In 1851 he bought Lochalsh, the ancestral possessions of his House, for £120,000. In 1857 he acquired Strathbran and Ledgowan, near Achnasheen, for £32,000. In 1861, Attadale, the last heritable property in the hands of his ancestors, he secured for £14,520, and in 1866 he bought New Kelso and Strathcarron for £26,000 ; altogether a magnificent stretch of Highland property, containing about 115,000 acres, at a total cost of £238,020, which in 1881 realised an annual rent of £13,705. In addition to the original cost, Mr Matheson has since spent about £120,000, including some £50,000 expended on his beautiful mansion of Duncraig, on the improvement of his West Highland property, bringing the total up to £358,020.

During the same period that he was accumulating this large property in the west, he acquired the estate of Ardross, extending to 60,000 acres, in Easter Ross, at a cost of £90,000; Dalmore, for £24,700; Culcairn, for £26,640; Delny and Balintraid, for £28,250; which, with other neighbouring properties, make a sum, for lands in Easter Ross, amounting to over £185,000, yielding an annual rental, in 1881, of £9324; while the outlays for improvements, including Ardross Castle and grounds, amount to nearly £230,000; total, £415,000. His entire possessions in the County of Ross extend to over 220,000 acres at a total cost of £773,020.

In addition to these extensive and valuable estates, Mr Matheson, in 1847, purchased lands in the Burgh of Inverness— the most valuable portion of the estate of Muirtown, and the smaller properties of Fairfield, Planefield, Macleod's Park, and Ness House Grounds, lying between the River Ness and the Caledonian Canal, and including all the feu-duties and the greater part of the feuing-ground present and prospective (except the property of the Mackintosh Farr Trustees), on the west side of the Ness. In addition to the purchase price of this property, Mr Matheson has spent between £35,000 and £40,000 in improvements and modern buildings on the estate, the rental of which, in 1881, was about £3,500, but which by no means represents the ultimate value of the property, which is yearly increasing from new feu-duties. The rental in 1862 was only £1141, but by purchase of the small properties above-mentioned, and the judicious outlay on roads and buildings, under the wise management of Mr Alex. Ross, architect, Inverness, the property is daily getting very much more enhanced in value.

In 1875, on the occasion of the coming of age of Kenneth J. Matheson, his heir, we are told that "it is no disparagement to other lairds to say that Mr Matheson was among the first in the present generation who saw the advantage of acquiring Highland property as a means of employing capital advantageously in the development of the resources of the country, and it is only due to patriotic feeling to point out the care with which, in the revolution which his improvements have effected in many parts of the County of Ross, he has avoided disturbing the traditional associations of the people. Something like £300,000 has been expended by Mr Matheson in land improvements and building in Ross-shire, but in all the work which that vast sum represents, we have not heard that it was found necessary to embitter the feelings of a single township, or even a shealing. His capital has been used to the great benefit of the country, and the means employed have been administered with so much wisdom, forbearance, and kindliness, that the demonstrations of rejoicing now agitating the County of Ross are, we believe, as sincere and hearty as they are universal."* In all this we heartily concur.

The improvements on the Ardross property have been on a most extensive scale. When it came into the possession of Mr Matheson it had a population of 109 souls. The place itself is described as "a rough, undeveloped piece of mountain land," while "innumerable boulders of the coarsest porphyry strewed the hillsides, and were buried in the bogs that covered the low-lying lands." The result of the improvements is described as marvellous. "About 5000 acres have been put under wood; 4000 acres have been brought into cultivation, and rarely have been seen pasture and corn fields giving richer promise of an abundant harvest than the large, well-fenced enclosures between Alness and Ardross. There is now [1875] a population of about 500 or 600 people on the property, twenty to thirty of them being substantial farmers." In the short period of nine years the improvements on this one estate comprised the trenching, draining, and liming of 2600 acres, the building of 67½ miles of dykes, the erection of 11 miles of wire-fencing, the making of 28 miles of roads, and the planting and enclosing of 3000 acres, besides the erection of new steadings, and the building of a magnificent modern castle, with all its adjuncts, all on a scale and in a spirit previously unexampled in the Highlands.

The late factor, Mr William Mackenzie, writing in the *Transactions of the Highland Society* in 1858, says:—"It was not the wish of Mr Matheson that any of the old tenants should leave the property; he was anxious and willing to provide them all with good farms and far better houses than they ever had," but these should be within the general scope of the improvements. " Indeed upon the whole of Mr Matheson's extensive possessions there has been no clearing of the old inhabitants to make room for improvements or sheep walks. It has been found perfectly compatible to carry out the most extensive improvements without removing a single tenant, or attempting to expatriate a peasantry of which any country might be justly proud. All that has been

* *Inverness Courier*, May 1875.

found necessary was simply to adjust matters; and none can be more easily managed than our Highland crofters in this way, if they are but kindly and fairly dealt with." Mr Matheson and his subordinates appear to have acted throughout on this wise and patriotic principle of kindness and fair-dealing.

He was not only instrumental in getting the Dingwall and Skye Railway constructed, but it is doubtful whether, without his influence and means, we should have had even yet a railway across the Grampians connecting us directly with the South. There is no doubt at all that to him and to the Duke of Sutherland is mainly due that we have a system of railways throughout the Highlands, and the consequent prosperity which has followed in its wake during the last twenty years.

Mr Matheson is and has been for years Chairman of the Highland Railway. He represented the Inverness District of Burghs in Parliament from 1847 to 1868, when, on the retirement of his uncle, Sir James Matheson of the Lews, from the County of Ross, Mr Matheson gave up the Burghs and succeeded his uncle in the representation in Parliament of his native county, a position which he still holds.

This year his public services have been suitably acknowledged by the Crown, a Baronetcy having just been conferred upon him. On the 12th of May last he was gazetted Sir Alexander Matheson, Baronet, of Lochalsh.

He married, first, in 1840, Mary, only daughter of James Crawford Macleod, Younger of Geanies, without issue. She died in 1841. He married, secondly, in 1853, the Honourable Lavinia Mary (who died in 1855), youngest daughter of Thomas Stapleton of Carlton, Yorkshire, and sister of Miles, 8th Lord Beaumont (descended from Miles, first Lord Stapleton—who died in 1314—by Sibill, eldest daughter of Sir John de Bella Aqui, or Bellew, heiress of Carlton; and also from John, second Lord Beaumont—who died in 1342—by Lady Alianora Plantagenet, daughter of Henry Earl of Lancaster, and great-granddaughter of Henry III., King of England.) By this lady Mr Matheson has issue—

1. Kenneth James, his heir, now Younger of Lochalsh; born in 1854.
2. Mary Isabell, who, in 1881, married Wallace Charles

Houston, youngest son of the late Col. Houston of Clerkington.

Mr Matheson married, thirdly, in 1860, Eleanor Irving (who died in 1879), fifth daughter of Spencer Perceval (by Anna, daughter of General Norman Macleod of Macleod), and granddaughter of the Right Hon. Spencer Perceval, Prime Minister of Great Britain (assassinated in 1812), son of John, second Earl of Egmont. By this lady, his third wife, Mr Matheson has issue—

3. Alexander Perceval, born in 1861.
4. Roderick Mackenzie Chisholm, born in 1861.
5. Farquhar George, born in 1871.
6. Eleanor Margaret; 7. Anna Elizabeth,
8. Flora; 9. Hylda Nora Grace.

THE MATHESONS OF SHINESS, ACHANY, AND THE LEWS.

IT has been already pointed out [p. 8] how, in the fifteenth century,

DONALD BAN MATHESON, son of Alexander Matheson of Lochalsh, fled to Caithness and became progenitor of this family. It is said that the Chancellor of Caithness was, at the time, a Matheson, and that this accounts for Donald's choice of that remote country when he had to find protection from his step-father, Macleod, who was lording it so haughtily in Lochalsh. By a daughter of the Earl of Caithness Donald Bàn had a son who, according to the tradition recorded in all the Matheson manuscripts, was born in Lochalsh.* The son was named

JOHN MATHESON, but he was better known among the Highlanders as "Ian Gallach," or John of Caithness, and his descendants to this day are sometimes called "Sliochd Ian Ghallaich," or the descendants of John of Caithness. He settled on the lands of Shiness, which extended along the North-east side of Loch Shin, in Sutherlandshire. He was succeeded by his son,

JOHN MATHESON of Shiness, referred to in Sir Robert Gordon's Earldom of Sutherland, as one who, in 1569, with Y. Mackay, made a narrow escape from a fearful snow-storm on a certain foray. He is described as "John Mak-ean Mak-Konald wain [John son of John, son of Donald Bàn], who dwelleth now in Cinenes [Shiness], and is at this day [1639] Cheiff of the tryb of Seilwohan [Siol Mhathoin] in Southerland." This is the first authentic glimpse we obtain of this branch of the Mathesons; and so little is known of John's successors that it will be impossible to give more than a very incomplete genealogical sketch of his descendants.

In 1579 several of the leading men of the district were surprised and killed at Durness by the Chief of the Aberigh Mackays and others, at the instigation of the Earl of Caithness, because these leaders gave allegiance to the Earl of Sutherland,

* See footnote, p. 8.

"at which tyme John Mack-ean-Mack-Donald-Wane* in Cinenes (cheiftane of the Scillwohan) escaped with great valor through the midst of his enemies, being then in the company of John Beg Mackay."

A tribe of the Mackenzies, known as "Siol Thomais," originally from Ardmeanach, in Ross-shire, obtained a strong footing in Sutherlandshire by the aid of the "Siol Wohan," or Mathesons, who appear to have followed the lead of the Mackenzies until January 1616, when, on the recommendation of Sir Robert Gordon, Tutor of Sutherland, they elected a chief of their own in the person of John Matheson, and separated from the Mackenzies. Sir Robert's namesake, the author of *The Earldom of Sutherland* [pp. 326-27], gives the following account of how this election came about. Sir Robert, "perceaveing that some of Scill-Thomas in Southerland began now to depend vpon Macky (alledging ther tryb to be descended of his house, although ther begining and first predicessors came out of Ardmeanagh in Rosse), he essayed to weaken the power of the Seill-Thomas, becaus he thought it a dangerous exemple that any tryb within that cuntrey should depend vpon any other then the Earle of Southerland, or such as did supplie his place, which he brought to pass in this manner: There is a race of people in Southerland, of equall, yea rather of greater force and power than the Seill-Thomas called Scill Wohan. This clan, or tryb, at all meetings, conventions, weapon-shews, and hoisting, these many years bypast still joined themselves to the Scil-Thomas; so that now they were both almost reputed to be one familie, under the name of Seil-Thomas. Sir Robert thought iff he could withdraw the concurrance and assistance of this people from the Scil-Thomas, that then the Scil-Thomas wold be of little force. Therefor he taketh occasion to send for the tryb of Scil-Wohan, and declared vnto them how far more honorable it were for the Earle of Southerland, and greater credet for themselves to choyse a chieftane or captane of ther owne tryb, then thus to give their attendance to others, who were their inferiors, and at the most, bot ther equalls: that they were as strong everie way as the Scil-Thomas, and therefore he advysed them to choyse a heid of ther owne race and familie, who wold be, from tyme to tyme, ansuerable for the rest of his

* John Mac Ian Mac Dhomhnuill Bhàin.

tryb to the Earle of Southerland, or to any haveing his place: that so they should not onlie be in greater accompt with their lord and master, the Earle of Southerland, bot lykwise therby they should be more respected by the rest of the inhabitants within the cuntrey. Whervnto they hearkned willinglie, and the motion pleased them weill; so they did choyse John Mack-ean-Mac-Konald Wain, in Chinenes, for head and chiftane of ther tryb; which policie of Sir Robert's hath much weakned the power of the Seil-Thomas." Matheson must have lived to a good old age, for, as we have seen, he is referred to by Sir Robert Gordon as being very prominent among the leading men of Sutherland in 1569 and 1579; or 47 years earlier than 1616, when he was elected chief.

He was succeeded by his son,

GEORGE MATHESON of Shiness, who, in 1626, accompanied Sir Donald Mackay of Farr, afterwards Lord Reay, to the wars of Gustavus Adolphus, King of Denmark, in whose service he rose to the rank of Colonel. He, on his return, on the 5th of October 1639, matriculated his arms, in the Lyon Office, describing himself as Colonel George Matheson. The next head of the family of whom we know anything after Colonel George, and who must have been his grandson or great-grandson, is

DONALD MATHESON, who took an active part on the side of the Government in 1715. Donald was succeeded by his son,

NIEL MATHESON, born in 1740, and, at the head of his house, in 1745-46. His son, Duncan, however, seems to have represented his father in the field, and fought against the followers of Prince Charles Edward. In a skirmish with the enemy, the latter received a wound, from the effects of which he died, in 1750.

Duncan married Elizabeth, daughter of William Mackay of Moudel, with issue—(1) Donald, who succeeded his grandfather; and (2) a daughter, Anne, who died young. After Duncan's death his widow married Dr Archibald Campbell, by whom she had issue, among others—George Washington Campbell, Secretary to the Treasury of the United States of America, and afterwards Ambassador-Extraordinary to the Russian Court at St Petersburg. Niel Matheson outlived his son, Duncan, for 25 years, and on his own death, in advanced years, in 1775, he was succeeded by his grandson,

DONALD MATHESON, then in the twenty-ninth year of his age. In 1762, in his sixteenth year, he was appointed Ensign in a Fencible Regiment, raised by the Earl of Sutherland in 1759, and served with it until the peace of 1763, when the regiment was disbanded. The Earl raised another Fencible Regiment in 1779, and Matheson joined it as Captain-Lieutenant. This corps was reduced at Fort-George in 1783.

Matheson married, in the same year, Catherine, daughter of the Rev. Thomas Mackay, minister of Lairg, by his wife, Catherine, daughter of John Mackay, Kirtomy, and grand-daughter of James Mackay, nephew of Donald, first Lord Reay, by his wife, Jean, daughter of the Hon. Sir James Fraser of Brae, son of Simon, eighth Lord Lovat. By this lady Donald Matheson, at his death, in 1810, left a family of three sons and five daughters—

1. Duncan, his heir, born in 1784.

2. James Sutherland, afterwards of the Lews. He was born at Lairg, Sutherlandshire, in 1796. Educated at the High School and at the University of Edinburgh, he afterwards joined the well-known mercantile house of Jardine, Matheson, & Co., of India and China, where he amassed a large fortune. As a partner of this firm he resided for many years abroad. On the occasion of his return to his native country, in 1842, he was presented by the native merchants of Bombay with a service of plate of the value of £1500, with an address, in acknowledgment of his exertions in promoting British commerce during the first Chinese war, and for his conduct during the Opium dispute with the Celestial Empire. He published a pamphlet on the position and prospects of the China trade, which secured considerable attention; was elected a Fellow of the Royal Society; and represented Ashburton in Parliament from 1843 to 1847. In the latter year, he was elected for the Counties of Ross and Cromarty, which he continued to represent until he resigned in 1868. In 1843, he had married, Mary Jane, fourth daughter of Michael Henry Perceval of Spencer Wood, Canada, a member of the Legislative Council of Quebec (who survives him), without issue. In 1851 he was created a Baronet of the United Kingdom in recognition of his great exertions and munificence in providing the inhabitants of the Lews (which Island he had previously purchased from Mrs Stewart-Mackenzie of Seaforth) with food during

the severe famine of 1845-46 and succeeding years. He spent an amount of money on building his residence, Lews Castle, laying out the grounds, and on improving his property generally, which, in any previous era of Highland history would have been considered fabulous; but the manner of this expenditure, and its results generally throughout the Island, as well as the career of Sir James generally in the Commercial world, and as a landed proprietor and public man, will demand a separate article.* In 1866 he was appointed Lord-Lieutenant of the Counties of Ross and Cromarty. He died, without issue, in 1878, leaving his Island principality, and the estate of Achany, Sutherlandshire, in life-rent to, and under the uncontrolled management of his widow, Lady Matheson of the Lews, and entailed on his nephew, Donald Matheson, present representative of the family of Shiness.

3. Thomas, a General in the army, born in 1798, and died unmarried in 1874.

4. Margaret, who, in 1804, married John Matheson of Attadale, and became the mother of Sir Alexander Matheson, Baronet, of Lochalsh, M.P. for the County of Ross, and several others.

5. Harriet, who, in 1814, married the Rev. Alexander Macpherson, D.D., minister of Golspie. She died in 1816.

6. Williamina, who died unmarried.

7. Johanna, now Miss Matheson of Achany, Sutherlandshire.

Donald Matheson of Shiness was succeeded as representative of the family by his eldest son,

DUNCAN MATHESON, an Advocate and Sheriff of the County of Edinburgh. He married, in 1815, Annabella, daughter of Thomas Farquharson of Howden, by whom (who died in 1829) he had issue—

1. Donald, his heir, born in 1819.

2. Hugh Mackay, who married Agnes, daughter of David Macfarlan, with issue—one son, Hugh, and two daughters.

3. Thomas, who, in 1850, married Anne, daughter of John Cropper, who died, leaving him no issue.

4. Elizabeth; 5, Isabella.

Duncan Matheson died in 1838, when he was succeeded, as representative of the family, by his eldest son,

* See Appendix.

THE MATHESONS.

DONALD MATHESON, who married, in 1849, Jane Ellen, third daughter of Horace Petley, Lieutenant, R.N., with issue—

1. Duncan, of the Inniskilling Dragoons, and who, born in 1850, married, in 1875, Clara Ellen, daughter of Sir Erasmus Dixon Borrowes, Baronet, with issue—a son, James Sutherland Mackay, born in 1880, and two daughters, Winifred Ellen, and another.

2. Donald, born in 1852.

3. James Horace, born in 1853.

He is the present representative of the Mathesons of Shiness, and heir of entail to the Lews and Achany estates of his late uncle, Sir James Matheson, Baronet, which are now held in life-rent by his widow, Lady Matheson of the Lews.

THE IOMAIRE MATHESONS.

THIS family claim descent from Alexander Matheson, alleged by his descendants to be the eldest son of John Matheson of Fernaig. If this contention were maintained, the chiefship of the whole Clan Matheson would necessarily fall to this family. We have already [p. 16] indicated our opinion on this point. According to the "Iomaire" Manuscript, where the claim is seriously made,

ALEXANDER MATHESON, who lived in Duriness, Lochalsh, married Isabella, daughter of Murdoch, son of Hector Mackenzie of Fairburn, with issue, four sons—

1. Roderick, his heir.
2. Duncan, married, without male issue.
3. Murdoch, and 4, Angus, both of whom were drowned on their way to the Isle of Skye.

He was succeeded by his eldest son,

RODERICK MATHESON, who married Flora, daughter of Alexander Matheson, known as "Alastair Mac Ian Oig," in Achataytoralan, with issue—

1. John, his heir.
2. Alexander, who married a daughter of John Mackinnon in Strath, Isle of Skye, by whom he had a numerous issue, long ago extinct in the male line.
3. Murdoch, who married Flora, daughter of John, second son of Alexander Matheson, "Alastair Mac Ian Oig," in Achataytoralan, with issue several sons and daughters, all of whom died young, except one son, Alexander, afterwards Rector of the High School of Edinburgh; and one daughter, Anne, who married William Macdonald, Ord, afterwards tinsmith in Dalkeith.
4. Donald, who married one of the Mackenzies of Hilton. He resided in the Parish of Contin, where he left two sons—Donald and Alexander—where both of them were alive in 1824.
5. Annabella.

He was succeeded by his eldest son,

JOHN MATHESON, who married Mary, daughter of Duncan (second son of Kenneth Mackenzie of the family of Davochmaluag) by his wife, Janet, daughter of Lachlan Mackinnon, Breakish, Isle of Skye, better known as "Lachlan Mac Thearlaich Oig," the well-known Gaelic poet. Lachlan's mother was Marion, daughter of John Macleod of Drynoch.

John Matheson was tacksman of Inchnairn, in Achamore. He died young, leaving issue, by his wife as above, two boys—

1. Alexander, his heir.

2. Murdoch, who married, and had four sons, all of whom died young, except Donald, the youngest, who was, in 1824, schoolmaster in Ardgour, Lochaber, where he married, with issue—(1) Alexander, who resides near Edinburgh, and married a lady of the family of Colonel Macdonald of Powderhall, with issue—three sons and three daughters. He died in 1880. (2) Murdoch, residing at Castleton, Braemar, who married Helen Gunn, with issue—two sons and three daughters; and (3) a daughter.

John Matheson was succeeded by his eldest son,

ALEXANDER MATHESON, who married Janet, daughter of Duncan Macrae, Tutor of Conchra, by his wife, Isabella, daughter of Finlay Macrae, minister of Lochalsh, by his first wife, Margaret, daughter of Duncan Macrae of Inverinate, by his wife, Janet Macleod of Raasay. It is said that none of the Mathesons of the West followed Bennetsfield at the battle of Culloden, which is pointed to as evidence that they did not acknowledge him as chief of the whole clan. This Alexander accompanied his clansmen from Lochalsh, though only in his eighteenth year. While retreating from the field Cumberland's dragoons overtook them, and two of the enemy, who were considerably in advance of the others, were, by a preconcerted arrangement, allowed to come in at the gallop, but no sooner had they got past the first rear man than the horses' ham-strings were cut, and the dragoons despatched without ceremony. The rest of the troopers, seeing their leading comrades fall, turned back, and the retreating Mathesons, among whom Alexander was prominent, saw them no more. One of the saddles was taken home by Matheson and was carefully preserved for many years, until it was torn to pieces by a youth of the family, who had no idea how interesting and valuable the article was to the antiquarian and to the elders of his own house. Alexander Matheson lived at Sallachy, Lochalsh, where he died in 1793, leaving by his wife, Janet Macrae, one son,

THE MATHESONS.

RODERICK MATHESON, known as "Ruairi 'n Iomaire," the author of the Iomaire manuscript, to which we are indebted for particulars of the family. He married Margaret, daughter of Finlay Macrae, descended on the father's side from Alexander Macrae of Inverinate, and, on the mother's, from Donald Macrae of Torloisich, who fell at Sheriffmuir in 1715. By her Roderick had issue seven sons and six daughters—

1. John, who married Mary Stalker, with issue—(1) Alexander, who succeeded his grandfather as representative of the family. He emigrated to America, but afterwards returned to Scotland, and died at Bridge of Allan, unmarried; (2) John, in Glenshiel, who married Christina Munro, Fearn, with issue—Roderick, who lives at home, and John, who has gone to America; (3) Murdoch, married, in Glasgow, with issue—one son, John, and two daughters; (4) Janet; (5) Mary; (6) Anne; (7) Flora. John died before his father in July 1822.

2. Alexander, who died unmarried.

3. Murdoch, who was educated at King's College, Aberdeen, went to America in 1809, and died, unmarried, at Lexington, Georgia, on the 12th of September 1817, where a monument is erected to his memory.

4. Duncan, who married Janet Macrae, with issue—Donald, in Lochalsh, married, with issue—Donald, in the Long Island, and two daughters, Flora and Annabella, both married, in Lochalsh.

5. Farquhar, who married Catherine Matheson, with issue—(1) Roderick, in the Inland Revenue, Edinburgh, married, with issue—three sons and a daughter; (2) Alexander, present parish minister of Glenshiel, still unmarried; (3) John, supervisor of Inland Revenue, Paisley, who married his cousin, Agnes Finlayson, with issue—five sons and four daughters; (4) Donald, Kirkton, Lochalsh, married, with issue—three sons and a daughter; (5) Murdoch, of the hon. Hudson Bay Company, who married, in March 1882, his cousin, Anne, daughter of the late John Macrae, Baintra, Lochalsh, and sister of Duncan Macrae, now of Ardintoul; (6) James, who died unmarried; and (7) a daughter.

6. William, who emigrated to Alabama. He married Maria Darrington, with issue—one son, William, who died unmarried, and three daughters.

7. Donald, who emigrated to America, and died unmarried.

8. Flora, who married Donald Maclennan, Plockton, where she died in 1820, leaving issue four sons and four daughters—John, Alexander, Kenneth, Murdoch, Janet, Elizabeth, Catherine, and Christina.

9. Catherine, who married John Mackintosh, Glenelg, without issue.

10. Isabella, who died young.

11. Janet, who married John Macdonell, Dornie, with issue—(1) Murdoch, who died unmarried; (2) John, who emigrated to America, where he died. He was married, and left issue in Scotland. (3) Roderick, who emigrated to New Zealand; (4) Dugald, who died young; and five daughters.

12. Annabella, who married Roderick Finlayson, Achamore, with issue—(1) John, who emigrated to New Zealand, where he recently died, unmarried; (2) Farquhar, in New Zealand, still unmarried; (3) Roderick, now tacksman of Achamore, married, with issue—several sons and daughters; (4) Duncan, supervisor of Inland Revenue, Kirkwall, who married Paulina Anne Sillick, a native of Burntisland, with issue—five sons and a daughter; (5) Flora, who married the late John Macrae, Braintra, with issue—*(a)* Duncan, present tacksman of Ardintoul; *(b)* Roderick, M.D., now resident surgeon at the Medical College, Calcutta. He went through the late Afghan Campaign. *(c)* Ewen, recently tacksman of Braintra, now in New Zealand; *(d)* Donald, a tea planter in Assam; *(e)* John, M.B., C.M., now in London; all of whom are still unmarried; *(f)* Anne, who married her cousin, Murdoch Matheson, of the hon. Hudson Bay Company, as above; (6) Mary, who married Alexander M'Erlich, Morar.

13. Anne, who died young.

He, Roderick Mackenzie, was succeeded, as representative of the family, by his grandson,

ALEXANDER MATHESON, who died, unmarried; when the representation of the family fell to the family of his brother,

JOHN MATHESON, Glenshiel, whose marriage and issue have been already given.

APPENDIX.

SIR JAMES MATHESON OF THE LEWS, BARONET.

UNDER the Mathesons of Shiness and Achany, in the county of Sutherland, we have referred briefly to this excellent man, and traced his descent through that family to the original Mathesons of Lochalsh. Sir James Matheson of the Lews, and his nephew, Sir Alexander Matheson of Lochalsh, are, perhaps, two of the most remarkably successful, and two of the best Highlanders, in many respects, of modern times. Unlike most men who have succeeded in the commercial world, and afterwards became landed proprietors, they have, altogether, treated their tenants as human beings, having different rights and higher claims on their consideration than mere articles of commerce. In their dealings with the people on their respective properties they have realised and given effect to the difference between men and women and bales of cotton or pig-iron. Such conduct, especially when the temptation and, probably, their personal interest were all in an opposite direction, ought to be recorded and highly commended.

We have already briefly stated what was done by Sir Alexander Matheson of Lochalsh, and we now proceed to record the more prominent acts in the career of his uncle, Sir James Matheson of the Lews, trusting that, in addition to the historical interest attached to such a useful life—his remarkable career—his rise and success in the world, by indomitable perseverance and sterling honesty alone, from a comparatively obscure position, may prove an example to others, not only in their efforts to get on in the world, but especially in the use they make of a good position after it is acquired by honest toil, persevering industry, and honesty.

Sir James was born, as already stated, at Shiness, in the parish of Lairg, county of Sutherland, on the 17th of November 1796. He was the second son of Donald Matheson, representative of the family of Shiness [see p. 52]. Having been educated, first, in the Royal Academy, Inverness, and afterwards in the High School and University of Edinburgh—where he had among his class-fellows the Right Hon. Sir David Dundas; David, Lord Marjoribanks; Sir Robert Christison, Baronet; Lord Brougham; and Anthony Adrian, Earl of Kintore—he determined to enter upon a commercial career, and to devote his energies entirely to it. He, at the age of seventeen, went to London; and, having spent two years in a mercantile house there, he, when only nineteen years old, proceeded to Calcutta, where he entered the counting house of Messrs Mackintosh & Co. After a short stay there he went to China, where he was long resident at Canton and Macao, and was one of the founders of the eminent and well-known house of Jardine, Matheson, & Coy., of Canton, and subsequently of Hong Kong.

A work, issued in Paris in 1844, entitled "The Historical and Biographical Annual of Foreign Sovereigns and Distinguished Personages," gives an interesting account of the commercial career of Sir James Matheson; and we cannot here do better than utilise a translation in our possession for a sketch of his life up to that period. According to this brochure the firm of Jardine, Matheson, & Company was "well-known for its extensive relations, the importance of its commercial operations, and the liberality of its acts. A great number of persons who, at the present moment [1844], enjoy all the pleasures of wealth might attest that they owe most of their prosperity to the gratuitous friendship and benevolence of Messrs Jardine, Matheson, & Co., who have always been ready to help liberally and disinterestedly. This is proved by the gratitude of the commanders and officers of the East India Company's ships who, when their commercial monopoly ceased in 1833-34, presented Mr Jardine, the senior partner of the firm, with a magnificent service of plate." It was not long after, however, before the services of Mr Matheson were also found of great value, and were ultimately suitably acknowledged in a similar manner.

For a few months Mr Matheson visited his native land in 1835-36, on which occasion he published a pamphlet on the state of commerce then, and its future, in China, which secured considerable attention; and the views which he then expressed, though disbelieved by many of his countrymen, proved his great insight and knowledge; for they were all fully confirmed by subsequent events.

In 1839, when serious differences arose between the British and Chinese Governments, Mr Matheson rendered most important services to the Civil authorities of his native country, as well as to the officers of the army and navy. It was owing to his mediation and influence at Canton, that Major Grattan of the 18th Regiment, Captain Dicey, and the officers and sailors of the East India Company's steamer *Madagascar*, which had been destroyed by fire on the Chinese coast, were set at liberty. They fell into the hands of the Chinese, but were released, during the war, in terms of a private arrangement entered into through the good offices of Mr Matheson.

He at all times used his influence to ameliorate the condition of the Chinese, and to establish various benevolent schemes in their interest. He was one of the most powerful supporters of Morrison's Educational Society, having for its principal object the teaching of English to the young Celestials. He also extended his influence and powerful aid in support of a Society established for the diffusion of useful knowledge among the natives; while he, at the same time, by every possible means, helped on the work of the successful missionary, Gutslaff, in several important and trying circumstances.

Mr Matheson was the first to introduce to China the benefits and active influence of a European Press. He imported from England a printing press, first, for his own amusement, but afterwards allowed its gratuitous use to establish and print, in 1827, the first English newspaper published in China, under the title of the *Canton Register*. This publication proved very useful to the Europeans in the Chinese Empire, supplying them with regular information of a trustworthy and most important character, enabling them, the more easily and rapidly, to understand Chinese affairs. The paper also contained translations from the best native works, and original articles by Mr Matheson's distinguished friend, the late Rev. Dr Morrison. The commercial department of the paper not only proved useful to and enlightened the Europeans, but also conveyed to the Chinese authorities a great amount of valuable information on various subjects, to them previously a sealed book. Mr Matheson subsequently, however, had cause to regret that this journal, instead of remaining in its original groove, became, under other management, an organ for violent personalities and political diatribes—a change of which he very much disapproved.

He was among the first to oppose the system of unjust exactions which then prevailed, and the bad treatment pursued by the local authorities, at Canton, towards those engaged in foreign commerce. He did what he could to expose all such proceedings whenever they occurred. He took a leading part in getting up the famous petition to the House of Commons, which Sir Robert Peel presented in 1830, and in which the English merchants of Canton fully stated their views and grounds of complaint.

In 1842 Mr Matheson decided upon returning to his native land, he having already amassed a splendid fortune. Before leaving he handed over 5000 Spanish dollars, or about £1120, to the Portuguese Government of Macao, for the establishment of some charitable institution; the English having resided in the town of Macao during the late war.

On his way home he called at Bombay, where the native merchants, headed by his old friend, Sir Jamsetjee-Jejebhoy, presented him with an address, and at the same time offered him a service of plate of the value of fifteen hundred pounds sterling, "in recognition of his wise and firm conduct during the difficult crisis preceding the Chinese War, when he had protected their commerce, on the occasion of the seizure of their opium. On the 13th of June, 1842, this address was presented to him in the house of Sir Jamsetjee-Jejebhoy, an old and valued friend, surrounded by a numerous and brilliant gathering, composed of men of different lands, races, and religions, who came forward from all directions with remarkable and unprecedented readiness and enthusiasm, "to express their gratitude to a man of such a great character, who, both as a merchant and philanthropist, merited so much public esteem, and whose liberality and munificence were indeed worthy of the title well bestowed upon him on this occasion of Merchant Prince." In name of the subscribers, and those present, Mr Framjee Comajee addressed Mr Matheson as follows: —"Your friends have been much grieved by the news of your intended return to England. They wish to express their grateful sentiments for the many acts of kindness and liberality which you have performed. They desire to express these in the Address which Mr Bomanjee Hormusjee is about to read." The last named gentleman then read the Address of the Parsee merchants of Bombay, which was couched in the following terms :—

My Dear Sir,—We cannot hear of your proposed return to England without feeling deeply grieved at the cause, which we hear is owing to the bad state of your health. We regret much to lose such a devoted friend, who supported our interests so successfully in times of incomparable difficulty and danger. During the space of three years, since the suspension of our commerce with China, we may state, without fear of contradiction, that any commerce of importance which we have been able to carry on has been entirely owing to your firmness and active perseverance. After the affair of the opium trade in 1839, which deprived India of two millions sterling, the Bombay trade was completely paralysed, and the most fatal consequences might have ensued; but you generously came to the rescue of our country and sustained our commerce, helping us to carry it on under foreign flags. All this was done at your own risk and on your own responsibility for the public welfare. When we consider what might have happened if you had not come to our assistance, we cannot express the measure of our gratitude to you. Our ships laden with cotton would have had to remain in the ports, the cargoes becoming rotten, while our fortunes would have been entirely destroyed. It is therefore natural that we, who are under such great obligations to you, and who owe so much to your wise conduct, should wish to express the great esteem we feel for your character and the gratitude we feel for your numerous acts of unparalleled liberality. We seize this opportunity with pleasure to express to you that we have had every reason to be grateful to you, and to state that we have never come to you with a reasonable request without its being received and granted by you with the greatest kindness. Our best wishes will always attend you, and in order to leave in your mind a perpetual souvenir of our affection, we have begged of our estimable friends, Messrs Magniac, Jardine, & Co., to present you, on your return to England, with a service of plate of the value of £1500, which we beg you to accept as a token of our sincere respect.

This address was signed by Cursetjee Ardusees Selt, Jamsetjee Jejebhoy, Jagonette Sunkersett, Dackjee Dadajee, Bomanjee Hormusjee, and 76 other equally distinguished native merchants of Bombay.

Mr Matheson returned thanks as follows :—

Dear Sirs,—The address which I have just had the pleasure of listening to is so flattering, and the offer which accompanied it so magnificent, that I feel quite overwhelmed at the honour you so kindly wish to do me, and I can find no words to express my great gratitude to you. I am quite convinced that the services you rate so highly are nothing more than a commercial agent owes to his correspondents. I can only attribute the fact that you deem these services worthy of such a great distinction, which I consider as very little merited, to the generous feelings which characterise your nation and dispose you to view any efforts made on behalf of your commercial interests in the most favourable light. This confirms the long experience I have had of your dealings, and is a great pleasure to me. The agent employed by you is always sure that, even were his efforts not crowned with success, they would be appreciated, and his conduct reviewed with indulgence, instead of, as is often the case, being made responsible for every result even if not favourable. This loyal confidence is what is most wanted to assist an agent, and it is that which caused us to act as we did in the unhappy circumstances which you mentioned on the occasion of the suspension of commerce in 1830. But I repeat that your indulgence causes you to rate these services too highly. We were guided by the simple rule of doing to others as we would wish to be done by, and, as the circumstances were extraordinary, extraordinary measures were necessary. I acted in common with the other partners of my house. The satisfaction which I feel at receiving this mark of esteem from such a large body of merchants is increased when I consider what an assembly of noble-minded men I have the pleasure of meeting to-day; when I think of your munificent charity, the means you have taken to help the indigent classes, the places of worship you have established, the hospitals you have opened, the schools and colleges you have founded to diffuse the knowledge and science of the Western world. Thus your loyal aid on behalf of every worthy institution is known to all; but my admiration is particularly excited by the knowledge I have of your private and constant charities, of which no one, I am sure, has an idea in Europe, and whose only reward is the approbation of your own consciences and that of the Invisible Being who governs the world. It would be an inexhaustible theme were I to enlarge on the estimable qualities of the Bombay merchants. I will only add that it is a great satisfaction to me, as well as to your other European friends, to know that your generous deeds have at last attracted the attention of our most gracious Soverign, who has given proofs of her appreciation by the honours borne by one of the members of your corporation. This is an important step towards the amalgamation of the interests of the two nations, England and India, and I am sure it is the precursor of other similar honours. There only remains now for me to express my deep gratitude to you for the honour you have wished to do me. Your splendid token of gratitude, precious in itself, will be doubly so on account of those by whom it is offered. I shall preserve it all my life, and it will be preserved by my heirs. Rest assured, however, that this present was not necessary to make me always remember you in my heart, whatever lot is reserved for me in China, in England, or elsewhere. I hope you will always consider me as your most devoted friend, and that you will never hesitate to ask any service from me. I shall always be most happy to be of any use to you. In conclusion, I wish you each every good fortune and happiness.

Before his return to Britain Mr Matheson, in 1840, purchased the estates of Achany and Gruids, in his native county of Sutherland, on which, including purchase price, he spent £91,000.

In 1847 he purchased the village of Ullapool from the British Fishery Commissioners at a cost of £5250, subject to a feu-duty of £50 10s, payable to the Countess of Cromartie, from whose ancestor, Lord Macleod, the Commissioners feued the estate in 1788. Sir James redeemed the feu-duty in 1878, for the sum of £1136.

In due course Mr Matheson arrived in Britain; and, in 1842, he was elected member of Parliament for Ashburton, Devonshire, of which town he was, jointly with Lord Clinton, lord of the Burgh and Manor. He soon became very popular with his constituents. Two thousand of the labouring classes of that burgh joined in a penny subscription, and presented him, during one of his visits, with a silver snuff-box, beautifully executed by Messrs Hunt & Roskell, of London.

Soon after his return to Britain he contributed a thousand pounds to the funds of the Royal Caledonian Asylum, London, and was then instrumental in opening up that excellent institution to girls, hitherto available to boys only. In addition to the handsome sum given by himself to the Asylum, he collected a considerable amount among his relatives and friends. Nor was he even thus early forgetful of his brother Highlanders in the North. The Academy of Tain, now a prosperous and high-class educational seminary, had been closed for some time for want of funds, but through Mr Matheson's personal munificence, and his influence among his friends, the Academy was placed in a good financial position, and reopened for the successful teaching of Highland youth in the higher branches of knowledge. In acknowledgment of this generous assistance and valuable service to the town and district, the Provost, Magistrates, and Town Council of Tain presented him with the Freedom of the Burgh. Mr Matheson also subcribed five hundred pounds towards the establishment of the Northern District Lunatic Asylum at Inverness, which has since proved such a blessing to the unfortunate creatures who previously wandered all over the country, in many cases unprotected and unprovided for, and, too often, to the great danger of the community.

In 1844 he purchased the Island of Lews from the Honourable Mrs Stewart Mackenzie of Seaforth for £190,000, and he entered into possession at Whitsunday of that year.

That the Seaforth Trustees might not harass his new tenants, he bought all the arrears due on the estate at Whitsunday, 1844, for which he paid a composition of £1417 18s 1d, and they were never charged against anyone, except in a few cases where feuars were in arrear who could well afford to pay their feu-duties.

This great Island principality has an area of some 417,469 acres, of which about 10,000 are arable. The original cost to Mr Matheson was about 9s 2½d, while the rental averaged

5¼d, per acre; the annual rent being, on the original capital invested, equal to £5 3s 1d per cent. The agricultural rental of the estate in 1844, when it came into Mr Matheson's possession, was £9,800. It is now £13,300, or an increase of £3,500, which must be placed against an outlay of £99,720 expended by the proprietor in building farm houses and offices, and on improvements and reclamations of land. Of the increased rental, £1,788 is derived from holdings of £15 and upwards, and £1,712 from crofters paying under £15 per annum.

Mr Matheson commenced his great efforts for the advancement of the material prosperity of the Island in 1845 by building a patent slip, quays, constructing roads, and other works for the promotion of trade, some of which have since proved of great permanent advantage, while others, unfortunately, have become complete and ruinous failures. His extraordinary efforts to improve the agricultural character of the Island have been great and earnest, though not, for various reasons, altogether successful.

The late Mr Smith, Deanston, who was at the time considered one of the most eminent of "speculative" agricultural authorities in Scotland, was engaged to survey the Lews with a view to improvements and reclamations of land, and he advised works on an extensive scale. He became Mr Matheson's adviser and engineer, and after surveying the whole island, he recommended the simultaneous prosecution of land reclamation on the coast and in the interior.

These works were commenced, in 1845, on six sections along the coast, and in one part of the interior 890 acres were reclaimed and brought under cultivation. These lands were thus apportioned:—In the Stornoway district, 520 acres; Loch Roag, 50; Galson, 140; Deanston, 60; Carloway, 40; Barvas, 40; and Shawbost, 40 acres. Part of the reclaimed lands in the Stornoway and Galson districts was added to existing holdings, all of which were then remodelled. The remainder was utimately divided among the crofters.

The test of Mr Smith's ambitious but ill-advised scheme was the portion of the interior upon which he operated, and which bears after him the name of Deanston, in the parish of Uig. The soil consisted of moss, from three feet to twelve feet in depth. Sixty acres were wedge-drained, and laid out in fields of 10 acres, enclosed with ditches and turf fences. The surface was dug by an operation something between the extremes of ploughing and trenching, after which a coating of clay marl was applied, followed by a good supply of shell sand, guano, and dissolved bones. Two of the fields were put through a course of arable cultivation, while the others were laid down in grass. Those fields were wrought for several years, and the driest part of the ground naturally gave a superior crop of grass. Afterwards this land was given to small crofters, but they had ultimately to abandon it, for, among other reasons, being too far from the sea coast, and, so, unable to procure sea-ware for manure or prosecute sea fishing in connection with their crofts, which by themselves were not large enough to support their families.

In 1850 the improvement scheme was suspended, and shortly afterwards given up altogether. In 1851, in spite of the noble efforts of the proprietor, four of the Parochial Boards of the Island sent a memorial to Lord John Russell praying the Government to afford relief in the shape "of a judiciously conducted emigration" to some of the many unoccupied tract of lands in the Colonies; and for aid for maintaining such members of the remanent population as might require it until the next crop became available. The memorial stated that all that had been expended by the proprietor "has proved unremunerative, and only in a small degree promotive of the existing or prospective comfort and prosperity of his tenants; that it is well known that the cereal produce of the Island has not, in the memory of man, been adequate to the supply of the inhabitants for more than four to six months of the year, and that the depreciation of all agricultural, pastoral, and fishing produce is 50 per cent." This memorial was forwarded by Sir James Matheson to Lord John Russell on 27th January, 1851, in a letter in which he endorsed the statements therein set forth, adding that "as the redundancy of population is notoriously the evil, emigration is the only effectual remedy to afford elbow-room and fair scope for the success of the antecedent measures which, from over population, have hitherto proved comparatively unavailing." Sir James was at this time spending a great deal more in the Island than the revenues from his estate. During the six years from 1844 to 1850, he spent, over and above his rental, the sum of £67,980, including, however, £29,124 borrowed from Government under the Drainage Act, for which some of the tenants paid 5 to 6½ per cent. interest, amounting in all to £561 18s 10d per annum.

The portions of land brought under cultivation nearest the coast have since been maintained in a crop-bearing state, and now yield a fair return. These improvements, at such enormous cost, have, however, to a large extent, turned out failures. To have employed a mere "speculative" agriculturist to carry them out, in a place like the Island of Lews, so different in every respect to the Lowlands of Scotland, was a misfortune, and an unfavourable result was inevitable from the beginning. For this, however, no blame can be attached to Mr Matheson. He was misled and imposed upon, and he had to pay for his error in a very substantial form. Referring to his laudable efforts to improve the condition of his people, the *Inverness Courier*, on the occasion of his death in 1878, says:—"Between 1844 and 1850, Sir James spent nearly £68,000 in improvements, and there is no more distressing example of the fruitlessness with which, for the most part, it was expended, than the township which Mr Smith called after his own place of abode in Stirlingshire. The soil is gradually relapsing into peat and heather, and the houses are falling back to the condition of the primitive natives of the Island. Still, the strongly-felt wish of the proprietor, that he should leave the island and its people better than he found them, has been in a great measure accomplished." In this all who know anything about the actual facts must concur.

In 1844, when Mr Matheson purchased the estate, there was no steam communication between the Island and the mainland. He immediately offered various firms of shipowners in Glasgow a subsidy of £500 annually to run a steamer between Glasgow and Stornoway, but no one agreed to undertake the risk, believing that no sufficient trade existed to support a steamer. He afterwards took shares in the "Falcon," a steamboat which ran for a short time between Ardrossan and Stornoway. This boat ceased running in October 1845, when Mr Matheson built, at his own expense, the "Mary Jane," soon found to be too small for the trade. The "Marquis of Stafford" was then built by him and the Duke of Sutherland for carrying on the business. She was, however, ultimately sold, when Mr John

Ramsay of Kildalton took up the traffic, and, after him, the well-known firm of Messrs David Hutcheson & Coy., now suceeeded by Mr David Macbrayne, who runs two steamers weekly to Stornoway. There is also, once a fortnight, a boat from Liverpool, Granton, Dundee, and Aberdeen; and during summer and harvest, one from Glasgow calls, once a month, in Loch Roag, on the west side of the Island.

Mr Matheson's loss by the "Falcon," "Mary Jane," and the "Marquis of Stafford" steamers amounted to £15,000.

Soon after his accession he built schools in almost every district of the Island, not previously provided for by a Parochial or Free Church school. Teachers from the Free Church Normal School were appointed and paid by him. These schools were not well patronised, and, after a few years' trial, Mr Matheson was so disappointed with the small attendance and with the little appreciation of the schools by the people, that he handed them over to the Edinburgh Ladies' Association, at the same time granting an annual sum towards the salaries of the teachers. He had also built, in Stornoway, an Industrial Seminary for females. Besides the ordinary branches of education, Ayrshire needlework was taught in this institution, but it was soon found that the latter did not pay, and it was ultimately given up. The seminary, however, is still upheld as an industrial institution by Lady Matheson. The outlay by Sir James on this institution and the other schools already mentioned—apart from grants to Parochial and Free Church schools—amounted to £11,681.

There are now not less than 32 Board Schools in the Island, in addition to 3, in the village of Stornoway, not under the Board, and 4, in outlying districts, maintained by the Edinburgh Ladies' Association.

In 1849, Mr Matheson was instrumental in forming a Gas company in Stornoway, in the capital of which he took £350. He also established a Water company, in which he invested £1,150.

When he purchased the property in 1844, there would have been about 45 miles of imperfectly formed, rough, country tracks in the Island. There are now over 200 miles of excellent roads, on which Sir James spent, including bridges, £25,593.

In 1845, there was but one solitary gig in the whole Island. There are now no less than 87 taxed conveyances.

When, in 1844, Mr Matheson came into possession, and for many years after, a sailing packet conveyed the mails twice a-week to and from Poolewe. Subsequently the steamers, as well as the sailing packet, carried the mails; and when Mr David Hutcheson placed two boats on the route, they carried the mails twice a-week, but still very irregularly. After many years' contending with the Post-Office authorities for a mail steamer to Stornoway, they at last offered to place the Lews on the same footing as the Orkney Islands, and offered a subsidy of £1,300 for the conveyance of the mails. No one could be found to take the contract at this price, and Sir James Matheson took it himself for a period of ten years, commencing on the 1st of August, 1871. By this arrangement he lost £16,805.

Between 1851 and 1861 no less than 1772 souls emigrated to Canada, while in the two succeeding years, 1862 and 1863, an additional band of 459 left for the same place, making a total, in twelve years, of 2231 from the Island. To pay their passage money to Quebec, their Canadian inland railway fares to the different settlements, and a considerable quantity of clothing and other furnishings, Sir James expended a sum of £11,855.

The population of the Lews in 1841, three years before it came into his possession, was 17,037; in 1851 it was 19,694; in 1861, notwithstanding the emigration stated, it increased to 21,056. In 1871 it reached 23,483; while in 1881 it amounted to 25,415 souls, in addition to 400 militamen who were out of the Island when the census was taken. This is a total of 2550 more than the whole population of the county of Sutherland, and an increase, since 1841, of 8788 souls, or more than 50 per cent.

There are at present in the Island of Lews 2881 crofters, paying a gross rental of £8,070 6s, or an average of £2 16s each.

To meet the great destitution of 1845-6, the proprietor imported meal and seed potatoes to the value of £33,000. About one-half of this sum was afterwards refunded by labour on roads or on other works of improvement.

In addition to the sums already stated, Sir James at one time or another expended the following sums:—

THE MATHESONS.

Castle Buildings and Offices, including Grounds and Policies	£100,495
Brickworks	6,000
Patent Slip	6,000
Fish-curing Houses	1,000
Bulls for Improvement of Crofters' Stock	1,200
Quay for Steamers at Stornoway	2,225
Chemical Works for Manufacturing Paraffin Oil from Peat	33,000
Cost and Outlay on Shooting Lodges	19,289
	£169,209

Sums already mentioned but not included in above statement:—

Buildings and Land Reclamation	£99,720
Industrial and other Schools	11,681
Gas Company	350
Water Company	1,150
Road and Bridges	25,593
Loss on Steamers	15,000
Loss on Contract for Carrying Mails by Steamer	16,805
Emigration of 2,231 souls to Canada	11,855
Meal, Seed Potatoes, &c.	33,000
	215,154
Original Cost of the Lews	190,000
Total Outlay by Sir James in the Island of Lews	£574,363

The gross rental from all sources, including £350, the sum at which the Castle and grounds are entered in the Valuation Roll, amounts to £19,154 3s 1d, and gives, in 1882, an annual gross return of £3 6s 6d per cent. From this, however, falls to be deducted the Public Burdens, amounting to £4027 17s 0d, which reduce the net return for this vast expenditure to £2 12s 8d per cent. per annum. But to give a more correct idea of the financial results of these operations, it is necessary to deduct the cost of Stornoway Castle, grounds, and policies, from the calculation on the one side, and the sum at which these are entered in the Valuation Roll for the county on the other, as these were in possession of the proprietor, and the expenditure on them bear no comparison with the sum entered against them in the Valuation Roll. The result is that the expenditure on the whole estate, apart from that on the portion of it in the hands of the proprietors themselves, gives a clear return of £3 2s 4d per cent. on the total purchase price and subsequent improvements—a very fair per centage, it will be admitted, as land goes.

Had this noble-minded and generous man placed less confidence in his subordinates the administration of the vast property under his charge would probably have been almost faultless, but like many more well-meaning and naturally generous landlords, he delegated too much responsibility to his factor, and this led to abuse in the latter years of his life, when he was unable from old age and failing health to give personal attention to the management of the property. Were it not for this we would never have heard of the "Bernera Riots." Sir James was a good, an excellent, and humane proprietor, generous and loyally trustful to a fault. He resided for eight or nine months each year in his Island home, among his people, who, during his life generally spoke, and still speak, of him in the highest terms.

In 1847 he retired from the representation of Ashburton, when he was unanimously elected for the combined counties of Ross and Cromarty, a position which he occupied to the entire satisfaction of his constituents until he retired into private life in 1868. He was appointed by Her Majesty, in 1866, Lord Lieutenant for the County of Ross. He was a Fellow of the Royal Society; and a J.P. and Deputy-Lieutenant of his native County of Sutherland.

In 1843 he married Mary Jane, fourth daughter of Michael Henry Perceval of Spencer Wood, Canada (a Member of the Legislative Council of Quebec), by his wife, Anne Mary, eldest daughter of Sir Charles Flower, Baronet, without issue. In 1850 Her Majesty testified to her sense of his benevolence during the Famine of 1845-46, by creating him a Baronet of the United Kingdom.

He died at Mentone, France, whither he had gone for the benefit of his health, on the 31st of December 1878, aged 82 years, and was buried at Lairg, in the county of Sutherland, where his widow, Lady Matheson of the Lews, erected a noble monument, with appropriate inscriptions, to his memory.

His estates are all left in life-rent to and under the uncontrolled management of Lady Matheson, and entailed on his nephew, Donald Matheson, present representative of the family of Shiness.

THE END.

www.ingramcontent.com/pod-product-compliance
Lightning Source LLC
Chambersburg PA
CBHW031608110426
42742CB00037B/1331